Skills for writing

Ann Mann
Codsall High School, Staffordshire
Hilary Rich
Newcastle-under-Lyme College, Staffordshire

Book 3   an examination course

Longman

Contents

Introduction

Each section of this book deals with a different type of writing.
The skills needed are listed at the beginning of each chapter.
The skills list shows you at a glance what the important areas
are. You can also use it as a checklist when preparing for an
examination.

The extracts have been chosen to give examples of a wide
range of writing styles and to draw your attention to ways in
which writers organise and express their ideas. The full range of
extracts, authors, and sources is on page 173.

From first draft to final copy

To produce your best work, you must be prepared to spend time **planning**, making a **first draft**, and **revising** it. Here are stages from a pupil's work.

The plan

What I can see	What I can hear	What I can smell/taste	What I can feel
Blackness at first small latticed windows sunlight -a ray furniture - chairs, bookcase, dust, cabinet, ornaments pictures on walls hanging curtains threadbare carpet wallpaper -faded and peeling	Silence Stillness Later a creaking door Own breathing	mustiness stale air dustiness dirt	dampness claustrophobia

The first draft

It was like entering another age.
It was so dark and dirty
looking and the quietness
struck me immediately, you could *grammar*
of heard any pin drop. A ray of
light came through the dirty *more interesting words needed*
grey windows. They were small
develop the idea of the light latticed windows and forced the
sun away from the room as if
showing the objects the room should not come alive.

V

The furniture was exquisit. sp.

change words— repeated big

The chairs were big and had big mahogany arm-rests. They were covered with a heavy material with big green flowers printed on. A Louis V chair was in the corner of the room,

think of more interesting words

deeply engraved down its thick legs. The curtains hung loosely from the windows over on the

unclear idea— change

otherside of the room stood a tall dark bookshelf full of old tattered books. There was dust everywhere and it had been ages since anyone had opened this room up. The intense musty smell was everywhere.

The second draft

It was like entering another age. It was dark, almost tomb-like, and the quietness immediately struck me. You could have heard a pin drop. The small latticed windows were grey with dirt and seemed to force the sun away from the room, as if it should not come to life. Slowly, a ray of light seeped through the dirt encrusted glass, and showed me something of the room. Curtains hung limply from the windows. There was dust everywhere.

The furniture was exquisite. The chairs were big and hefty with large mahogany arm-rests. They were covered with a heavy material decorated with green flowers. A Louis V chair, deeply engraved down its sturdy legs, sat peacefully in the corner of the room. On the other side of the room, stood a tall dark bookcase, full of old tattered books. Dust lingered everywhere, and an intense musty smell hovered about the room. It had been ages since anyone had opened it up.

Look at the first and final draft carefully. What changes have been made? How successful are they?
This method will help you produce your best pieces of work, which can be collected together to produce a folio of your writing.

1 Narrative writing

A narrative essay is one which tells a story. Some stories create mystery and suspense, some provide thrilling action, and others explore individual characters and their relationships. When you are writing a narrative, you must decide which of these is your aim and write in the appropriate style. Work out the main parts of the story so that the plot develops clearly. This involves writing a plan. Interest the reader from the beginning of the narrative, and keep that interest until the plot comes to its best conclusion.

How to begin

Decide on the content of the story, by answering these questions.

    Who are the main characters?

    What is the setting for the story?

    When does the story take place (time of day, season and year)?

    What is the plot to be?

In a narrative essay it is important that the **characters** are introduced, the **setting** and **time** of the story are made clear, and the **plot** is set in motion from the very beginning.

> Here are the openings of two stories. Read them carefully and answer the questions which follow.

The Green Suite

Mrs Farley was sitting in a bus when she first saw it. She spotted the price as the bus swerved round the corner and she wondered if it could be possible. A three-piece suite covered in dark green tapestry. Second hand, of course, but not so shabby that you'd know. After all, it could be one that she'd had in her house for years, ever since she married. She'd buy it.

Luckily she had a pound in her purse which served as a deposit. While the man wrote out a receipt she sat on the armchairs, then on the couch, moving along the seat to make sure it was thoroughly sprung. How well it would fit in her front room. In the evening, she and Mr Farley would have an armchair each. In May when Mr Farley went on the boiler-makers' outing, she and her friend would share the couch.

It would be perfect. May ... the sun through the windows shining on the caster-oil plant, and the couch a darker shade of green with anti-macassars to protect from sun and greasy hair. There would be a cushion for behind his back, and with a bit of luck some things would be in bloom, disguising the creosote-soaked fence. He would see what a good gardener she was.

from *An Outing* by Edna O'Brien

A Loaf of Bread

It was a cheerless morning, the sky was overcast with grey opaque vapour like a veil. Every third person or so that you passed in the street coughed, and each one seemed as dispirited as the next. You saw the sadness of people now, even under the casual laughter and the bravado of indifference.

Old Ben walked along without looking to the right or left of him, and the boy pattered along behind. He had forgotten that he had not had any breakfast, and that he was hungry. He walked with the sort of aimless desperation of a man who has nowhere to go; but it seemed to him necessary, although barren of result.

The boy, uncomplaining, walked always a little behind; reminded old Ben of his presence by suddenly giving way to a fit of coughing, precipitated by that tickling burning feeling in his throat. Ben stopped, suddenly remembered the boy and breakfast; remembered that Tim must be hungry; thinking suddenly of hunger, emptiness his own loss, and his emptiness in a world of emptiness, passing from one bleak façade to the next, a shop.

They went inside, and Ben bought a threepenny loaf of bread, paid threepence more and the Chinaman obligingly cut the loaf right in two down the middle lengthwise and smeared butter on both sides facing, clamped them together shut, and Ben taking, broke the loaf in two, passed one portion to the boy.

They left the shop, walking the streets again, eating their breakfast as they went.

from *World's End* by Roger Mais

Questions

1 From each extract explain what you found about:
 – the main characters
 – the setting for the story
 – when the story takes place.
2 Using the clues given in these opening paragraphs, explain what you think the rest of each story will be about.
3 What type of story would each of these extracts introduce?

Planning a story

Read the following story carefully. Then answer the questions, which will help you learn how to plan.

Examination Day

The Jordans never spoke of the exam, not until their son, Dickie, was twelve years old. It was on his birthday that Mrs Jordan first mentioned the subject in his presence, and the anxious manner of her speech caused her husband to answer sharply.

'Forget about it,' he said. 'He'll do all right.'

They were at breakfast table, and the boy looked up from his plate curiously. He was an alert-eyed youngster with flat blond hair and a quick, nervous manner. He didn't understand what the sudden tension was about, but he did know that today was his birthday, and he wanted harmony above all. Somewhere in the little apartment there were wrapped, beribboned packages waiting to be opened, and in the tiny wall-kitchen something warm and sweet was being prepared in the automatic stove. He wanted the day to be happy, and the moistness of his mother's eyes, the scowl on his father's face, spoiled the mood of fluttering expectation with which he had greeted the morning.

'What exam?' he asked.

His mother looked at the tablecloth. 'It's just a sort of Government Intelligence test they give children at the age of twelve. You'll be taking it next week. It's nothing to worry about.'

'You mean a test like in school?'

'Something like that,' his father said, getting up from the table. 'Go and read your comics, Dickie.' The boy rose and wandered towards that part of the living room which had been 'his' corner since infancy. He fingered the topmost comic of the stack, but seemed uninterested in the colour-ful squares of fast-paced action. He wandered towards the window, and peered gloomily at the veil of mist that shrouded the glass.

'Why did it have to rain today?' he said. 'Why couldn't it rain tomorrow?'

His father, now slumped into an armchair with the Government newspaper rattled the sheets in vexation. 'Because it just did, that's all. Rain makes the grass grow.'

'Why, Dad?'

'Because it does, that's all.'

Dickie puckered his brow. 'What makes it green, though? The grass?'

'Nobody knows,' his father snapped, then immediately regretted his abruptness.

Later in the day, it was birthday time again. His mother beamed as she handed over the gaily-coloured packages, and even his father managed a grin and a rumple of the hair. He kissed his mother and shook hands gravely with his father. Then the birthday cake was brought forth, and the ceremonies concluded.

An hour later, seated by the window, he watched the sun force its way between the clouds.

'Dad,' he said, 'how far away is the sun?'

'Five thousand miles,' his father said.

Dickie sat at the breakfast table and again saw moisture in his mother's eyes. He didn't connect her tears with the exam until his father suddenly brought the subject to light again.

'Well, Dickie,' he said, with a manly frown, 'you've got an appointment today.'

'I know Dad. I hope –'

'Now, it's nothing to worry about. Thousands of children take this test every day. The Government wants to know how smart you are, Dickie. That's all there is to it.'

'I get good marks in school,' he said hesitantly.

'This is different. This is a – special kind of test. They give you this stuff to drink, you see, and then you go into a room where there's a sort of machine –'

'What stuff to drink?' Dickie said.

'It's nothing. It tastes like peppermint. It's just to make sure you answer the questions truthfully. Not that the Government thinks you won't tell the truth, but it makes *sure*.'

Dickie's face showed puzzlement, and a touch of fright.
He looked at his mother, and she composed her face into a
misty smile.

'Everything will be all right,' she said.

'Of course it will,' his father agreed. 'You're a good boy,
Dickie; you'll make out fine. Then we'll come home and
celebrate. All right?'

'Yes sir,' Dickie said.

They entered the Government Educational Building fifteen
minutes before the appointed hour. They crossed the marble floors of the great pillared lobby, passed beneath an
archway and entered an automatic lift that brought them to
the fourth floor.

There was a young man wearing an insignia-less tunic,
seated at a polished desk in front of Room 404. He held a
clipboard in his hand, and he checked the list down to the
Js and permitted the Jordans to enter.

The room was as cold and official as a courtroom, with
long benches flanking metal tables. There were several
fathers and sons already there, and a thin-lipped woman
with cropped black hair was passing out sheets of paper.

Mr Jordan filled out the form, and returned it to the
clerk. Then he told Dickie: 'It won't be long now. When
they call your name, you just go through the doorway at
the end of the room.' He indicated the portal with his
finger.

A concealed loudspeaker crackled and called off the first
name. Dickie saw a boy leave his father's side reluctantly
and walk slowly towards the door.

At five minutes to eleven, they called the name of
Jordan.

'Good luck, son,' his father said, without looking at him.
'I'll call for you when the test is over.'

Dickie walked to the door and turned the knob. The
room inside was dim, and he could barely make out the
features of the grey-tunicked attendant who greeted him.

'Sit down,' the man said softly. He indicated a high stool
beside his desk. 'Your name's Richard Jordan?'

'Yes, sir.'

'Your classification number is 600–115. Drink this, Richard.'

He lifted a plastic cup from the desk and handed it to the boy. The liquid inside had the consistency of buttermilk, tasted only vaguely of the promised peppermint. Dickie downed it, and handed the man the empty cup.

He sat in silence, feeling drowsy, while the man wrote busily on a sheet of paper. Then the attendant looked at his watch, and rose to stand only inches from Dickie's face. He unclipped a penlike object from the pocket of his tunic, and flashed a tiny light into the boy's eyes.

'All right,' he said. 'Come with me, Richard.'

He led Dickie to the end of the room, where a single wooden armchair faced a multi-dialled computing machine. There was a microphone on the left arm of the chair, and when the boy sat down, he found its pinpoint head conveniently at his mouth.

'Now just relax, Richard. You'll be asked some questions, and you think them over carefully. Then give your answers into the microphone. The machine will take care of the rest.'

'Yes, sir.'

'I'll leave you alone now. Whenever you want to start, just say "ready" into the microphone.'

'Yes, sir.'

The man squeezed his shoulder, and left.

Dickie said, 'Ready.'

Lights appeared on the machine, and a mechanism whirred. A voice said: 'Complete this sequence. One, four, seven, ten . . .'

Mr and Mrs Jordan were in the living room, not speaking, not even speculating.

It was almost four o'clock when the telephone rang. The woman tried to reach it first, but her husband was quicker.

'Mr Jordan?'

The voice was clipped: a brisk, official voice.

'Yes, speaking.'

'This is the Government Educational Service. Your son, Richard M Jordan, Classification 600–115 has completed the Government examination. We regret to inform you that his intelligence quotient is above the Government regulation, according to Rule 84 Section 5 of the New Code.'

Across the room, the woman cried out, knowing nothing except the emotion she read on her husband's face.

'You may specify by telephone,' the voice droned on, 'whether you wish his body interred by the Government, or would you prefer a private burial place? The fee for Government burial is ten dollars.'

Henry Slesar

Questions

1 Describe how Dickie spends his twelfth birthday. How do his parents behave on this day?
2 On the day after his birthday, what is Dickie told about the test he is about to take?
3 What impressions are created of the place where the test is administered, and of the people who work there?
4 What happens to Dickie when it is his turn for the test?
5 What is the outcome of the examination?

Your answers to these questions give you the **main stages** of the story, which should be shown in a **plan**. When you construct a plan, use the most important points in the story as headings. You can then make detailed notes of the other points underneath.

The plan of examination day

DICKIE'S TWELFTH BIRTHDAY
At breakfast examination mentioned for
first time. Dickie waiting for presents
and cake. Parents seem anxious. Dickie tries
to occupy himself with comics etc. Eventually
celebrates his birthday.

EXAMINATION DAY
Day after birthday, Dickie to be taken for
the examination. Government test to see how
clever he is. Room, machine, truth drug.

EXAMINATION PLACE
Large building. Cold and official place.
People very officious and uncommunicative.
Tense atmosphere.

THE EXAMINATION
Number called at five to eleven. Father leaves.
Enters room. Given drink. Feels drowsy.
Computerised machine gives test. Questions
begin.

THE EXAMINATION RESULT
'Phone rings. Mr Jordan answers. Dickie did
too well. How do the family want him
buried?

Making a plan

> Read this story carefully, then answer the questions which follow. They will help you work out the main stages of the plot.

The Open Window

'My aunt will be down presently, Mr Nuttel,' said a very self-possessed young lady of fifteen. 'In the meantime you must try and put up with me.'

Framton Nuttel endeavoured to say the correct something which should duly flatter the niece of the moment without unduly discounting the aunt that was to come. Privately he doubted more than ever whether these formal visits on a succession of total strangers would do much towards helping the nerve cure which he was supposed to be undergoing.

'Do you know many of the people round here?' asked the niece, when she judged that they had had sufficient silent communion.

'Hardly a soul,' said Framton. 'My sister was staying here, at the rectory, you know, some four years ago, and she gave me letters of introduction to some of the people here.'

He made the last statement in a tone of distinct regret.

'Then you know practically nothing about my aunt?' pursued the self-possessed young lady.

'Only her name and address,' admitted the caller. He was wondering whether Mrs Sappleton was in the married or widowed state. An indefinable something about the room seemed to suggest masculine habitation.

'Her great tragedy happened just three years ago,' said the child; 'that would be since your sister's time.'

'Her tragedy?' asked Framton. Somehow in this restful country spot tragedies seemed out of place.

'You may wonder why we keep that window wide open on an October afternoon,' said the niece, indicating a large French window that opened on to a lawn.

'It is quite warm for the time of the year,' said Framton; 'but has that window got anything to do with the tragedy?'

'Out through the window, three years ago to a day, her husband and her two young brothers went off for their day's shooting. They never came back. In crossing the moor to their favourite snipe-shooting ground they were all three engulfed in a treacherous piece of bog. It had been that dreadful wet summer, you know, and places that were safe in other years gave way suddenly without warning. Their bodies were never recovered. That was the dreadful part of it.' Here the child's voice lost its self-possessed note and became falteringly human. 'Poor aunt always thinks that they will come back some day, they and the little brown spaniel that was lost with them, and walk in at that window, just as they used to do. That is why the window is kept open every evening till it is quite dusk. Poor dear aunt, she has often told me how they went out, her husband and his white waterproof coat over his arm, and Ronnie, her youngest brother, singing 'Bertie, why do you bound?' as he always did to tease her, because she said it got on her nerves. Do you know, sometimes on still evenings like this I almost get a creepy feeling that they will all walk in through that window . . .'

She broke off with a little shudder. It was a relief to Framton when the aunt bustled into the room with a whirl of apologies for being late in making her appearance.

'I hope Vera has been amusing you?' she said.

'She has been very interesting,' said Framton.

'I hope you don't mind the open window,' said Mrs Sappleton briskly. 'My husband and brothers will be home directly from shooting, and they always come in this way. They've been out for snipe in the marshes today so they'll make a fine mess over my poor carpets. So like you menfolk, isn't it?'

She rattled on cheerfully about the shooting and the scarcity of birds, and the prospects for duck in the winter. To Framton it was all purely horrible. He made a desperate but only partially successful effort to turn the talk on to a less ghastly topic. He was conscious that his hostess was giving only a fragment of her attention, and her eyes were constantly straying past him to the open window and the lawn beyond. It was certainly an unfortunate coincidence that he should have paid his visit on this tragic anniversary.

'The doctors agree in ordering me complete rest, and the absence of mental excitement and avoidance of anything in the nature of violent physical exercise,' announced Framton, who laboured under the tolerably widespread delusion that total strangers and chance acquaintances are hungry for the least detail of one's ailments and infirmities, their cause and cure. 'On the matter of diet they are not so much in agreement,' he continued.

'No?' said Mrs Sappleton, in a voice which only replaced a yawn at the last moment. Then she suddenly brightened into alert attention – but not to what Framton was saying.

'Here they are at last!' she cried. 'Just in time for tea, and don't they look as they were muddy up to the eyes!'

Framton shivered slightly and turned towards the niece with a look intended to convey sympathetic comprehension. The child was staring out through the open window with dazed horror in her eyes. In a chill shock of nameless fear Framton swung round in his seat and looked in the same direction.

In the deepening twilight three figures were walking across the lawn towards the window. They all carried guns under their arms, and one of them was additionally burdened with a white coat hung over his shoulders. A tired brown spaniel kept close at their heels. Noiselessly they neared the house, and then a hoarse young voice chanted out of the dusk: 'I said, Bertie, why do you bound?'

Framton grabbed wildly at his stick and hat. The hall door, the gravel drive and the front gate were dimly noted stages in his headlong retreat. A cyclist coming along the road had to run into the hedge to avoid imminent collision.

'Here we are, my dear,' said the bearer of the white mackintosh, coming in through the window; 'fairly muddy, but most of its dry. Who was that who bolted out as we came up?'

'A most extraordinary man, a Mr Nuttel,' said Mrs Sappleton: 'could only talk about his illness, and dashed off without a word of goodbye or apology when you arrived. One would think he had seen a ghost.'

'I expect it was the spaniel,' said the niece calmly. 'He told me he had a horror of dogs. He was once hunted into a cemetery somewhere on the banks of the Ganges by a pack of pariah dogs, and had to spend the night in a newly-dug grave with the creatures snarling and grinning and foaming just above him. Enough to make any one lose their nerve.'

Romance at short notice was her speciality.

Saki

Questions

1 Why does Framton Nuttel visit the Sappletons?
2 What reason does Vera give for the window being open on this particular October afternoon?
3 When Mrs Sappleton comes in, what does she say about the open window? What does this make Framton think about Mrs Sappleton's state of mind?
4 Why does Framton run away when he sees the men and the dog in the garden? What does Mrs Sappleton think about him?
5 What reason does Vera give for his behaviour? What does this show about Vera's character?

Practice work

Make a plan for this story similar to the one for *Examination Day*.

Opening paragraphs

The purpose of your opening paragraphs is to introduce the characters and to say what is necessary about time, place and setting. There are some **special techniques** you can use to make sure you do this in the most interesting way possible.

> You can begin **by describing the setting for the story in a way which creates atmosphere and expectation.**

The town woke, that long-anticipated January morning under a thin grey blanket of rain. From the upper slopes of the hills to the north the enveloping drizzle came swirling down to fold the worn-out Victorian villas, the square brown boxes on the new estate and the long terraces of dark stone houses in a uniform drabness. The narrow streets, around the handful of small factories that provided the sole reason for the town's existence, were murky chasms in the dim dawn. This was Saturday morning and the climax of the day's excitement was still several expectant hours in the future.

from *Cup Tie* by Gerald Sinstadt

Questions

1   What atmosphere does this description of the town create?
2   How does the writer encourage the reader to want to read on?

> You can begin **by surprising** the reader by describing something intended to shock.

John Woodford in his moments of returning consciousness was not aware that he was lying in his coffin. He had only a dull knowledge that he lay in utter darkness and that there was a close, heavy quality in the air he breathed. He felt very weak and had only a dim curiosity as to where he was and how he had come there.

He knew that he was not lying in his bedroom at home, for the darkness there was never so complete as this. Home? That memory brought others to John Woodford's dulled brain and he recalled his wife now, and his son. He remembered too that he had been ill at home, very ill. And that was all that he could remember.

from *The Man Who Returned* by Edmond Hamilton

Questions

1   What is John Woodford aware of when he wakes up?
2   What is he curious about?
3   How does this introduction shock the reader?

You can begin **by causing suspense**, and leave the reader wondering what happens next.

Only one thing puzzled Amelia Jenkyns about Number 109 Bolsover Square. It was this: why was the room at the end of the passage on the first floor always kept locked? Being superinquisitive, which was only one of her many failings, Amelia meant to find out.

She came from a waif and stray home in Peckham, where girls are to be got cheap. It was because of her cheapness that Mrs Bishop took her. Mrs Bishop was a widow, a blonde, whose yellow hair showed unmistakable signs of peroxide, and somewhere in the region of forty. She had big china-blue eyes with very artificial lashes, Greta Garbo eyebrows, and white hands, with tapering fingers and almond shaped nails, of which she was, perhaps, justifiably proud. Amelia thought her beautiful, but was afraid of her.

from *The Mystery of The Locked Room* by Elliot O'Donnell

Questions

1   How does the writer create an atmosphere of suspense?
2   What is the effect of the final sentence?

You can begin **by involving the reader straight away in the action of the plot**, as is shown in the following introduction.

The wind died away; in the complete silence he could hear the rapid beating of his own heart, then almost immediately below him, a stone rattled down and one breathing second later he heard footsteps ... slow, dragging, coming nearer. His breath seemed to stop; the hairs on his head prickled upright and his hands nearly let go their grip on the ruined parapet. The steps came nearer ... a light glimmered, pale and fitful, from the roofless stairway, shone faintly on the worn stone treads.

from *Brother Ramon's Return* by A. C. Stewart

Questions

1   What is happening at the start of the story?
2   What effect is this introduction intended to have on the reader?

Practice work

Here are the introductions to some stories. Read them carefully and decide what type of beginning is used in each.

1

Mr Elisha Peacock woke suddenly at four o'clock in the morning in the dead darkness, feeling very ill. For some moments immediately before waking he was aware of a strange sound of tinkling glass, of his whole body fighting a violent constriction in his chest. When he woke at last, it was some time before he realised that the sound was that of the night wind shaking the coloured glass chandelier above his head, that the conflict in his body was in reality a wire of pain boring down into his heart.

from *The Little Jeweller* by H. E. Bates

2

When Colin Sherrard opened his eyes after the crash, he could not imagine where he was. He seemed to be lying trapped in some kind of vehicle, on the summit of a rounded hill which sloped steeply away in all directions. Its surface was seared and blackened, as if a great fire had swept over it. Above him was a jet-black sky crowded with stars; one of them hung like a tiny brilliant sun, low down on the horizon.

from *Summertime on Icarus* by Arthur C Clarke

3

It all looked much smaller and shabbier than I remembered. From the top of Station Parade, I could see the town spread out below, grey and rather blurred in the fierce heat haze; punctuated here and there by the belching chimneys of the cement factories. It's a flat place. Only the station and the bleak cemetery occupy the single hill which protects them from the frequent danger of flood water.

from *Going Home* by Barry Davis

4

The morning of the great fire started, nobody in the house could put it out. It was Mother's niece, Marianne, living with us while her parents were in Europe, who was all aflame. So nobody could smash the little window in the red box at the corner and pull the trigger to bring the gushing hoses and the hatted firemen. Blazing like so much ignited cellophane, Marianne came downstairs, plumped herself with a loud cry or moan at the breakfast table, and refused to eat enough to fill a tooth cavity.

Mother and Father moved away, the warmth in the room being excessive.

from *The Great Fire* by Ray Bradbury

NARRATIVE WRITING

Practice work   Here are some first draft sentences written as openings to stories. Rewrite them keeping the basic meaning but making them much more interesting by using different styles of introduction.

1. The swimming pool was noisy. Everyone was pushing and shoving. Although some brave children jumped in quickly the scared ones stood shivering.

2. Jane had never got on well with her father and this time it was no different. She wanted a dog for her birthday but he said 'No'. This led to a serious quarrel.

3. When I was young it was during the war. Life was exciting then. Bombs used to go off during the night and we all had to go to the air-raid shelter for a long time. We used to wonder if our house had been hit.

4. As I waited at the time for the gun to go I felt nervous and sick. It was the big race. My chance to be a 'star' had come at last.

Write the opening paragraph for each of the following stories. Use a different type of introduction in each case – suspense, shock, beginning with the action.

The Power Cut
The Necklace
The Last to Go

18

Picture   Look at the pictures (on this page and the next) and write an introduction to each one creating the atmosphere.

Concluding paragraphs

The final paragraphs of a narrative essay must bring the story to a suitable conclusion. There are **different types** of conclusions which you can use.

> You can use a **positive ending**, by developing the plot to its obvious conclusion.

'It's me dad I'm feared for,' Shofiq said. His voice was odd; there was no tone to it, no expression, 'Maybe that Burke does believe what he's doing's right. Maybe he does think it's for our own good. But what will me dad do without me? What can he do? I've go to look after him, to help him. I'm the one that keeps the family going. What's going to happen to me dad?'

Bernard couldn't follow too well, but it seemed right. Wendy and Shofiq were staring at each other. They seemed to understand each other.

Wendy said: 'I'll tell them that, Shofiq. I'll do my best. I'll tell them that.' She rattled the front door one last time.

Shofiq said sadly: 'And d'you think they'll listen, Wendy? Do you?'

She made a funny little face, and took hold of Bernard's hand. With her other hand, the right one, she took hold of Shofiq's.

'Come on,' she said. 'Let's go and face the music.'

Shofiq looked at her, his big eyes bright and grave.

'Are you holding me to stop me running away?' he said quietly.

'Don't be daft,' said Wendy. 'You're Bernard's mate. I'm holding you because I like you. All right?'

A small smile appeared on Shofiq's face.

'Yes,' he said. 'All right.'

They went to face the music.

from *My Mate Shofiq* by Jan Needle

Questions

1 What clues are there to show what the plot of the story has been so far?

2 How is the plot drawn to its conclusion?

3 What is the effect of the final sentence?

You can end in **an unexpected way and shock or startle the reader.**

To the right a narrow ledge overhung a precipice at which she dared not look. To the left, on higher ground, a pile of stones ... on one of them a large black spider, spreadeagled, asleep in the sun. She had always been afraid of spiders, looked round for something with which to strike it down and saw Sara Waybourne, in a nightdress with one eye fixed and staring from a mask of rotting flesh.

An eagle hovering high above the golden peaks heard her scream as she ran towards the precipice and jumped. The spider scuttled to safety as the clumsy body went bouncing and rolling from rock to rock towards the valley below until at last the head in the brown hat was impaled upon a jutting crag.

from *Picnic at Hanging Rock* by Joan Lindsay

Questions

1   At the beginning of the extract, what is the woman's problem, and how does she intend to solve it?
2   What startles her, and how does she behave?
3   What is so shocking about this as an ending?

You can lead the reader to expect something very sensational to happen, but then 'let him down' with nothing really happening. This is **an anti-climax.**
Mr and Mrs Hutton are unhappily married. On this occasion he is particularly angry with her.

He wanted to see her coming in at the door. He wanted to see her weeping. He wanted to slam her against A WALLCHART OF SHAKESPEARIAN DRAMA, and smash her jaw and dabble in her blood.

But what good would it do? It wouldn't make him happy. It would wreck her. It would wreck Katie. He wished he hadn't found out. He wondered if he should kill himself, but he decided not to. He was too moral to die. What would the world be without him? He would live on a pillar of morality.

The bell rang. The Bechstein (piano) stopped. The first year stuck out their tongues at the prefects and clocked in. A C F Hutton sighed. He opened *A Midsummer Night's Dream*.

from *The Chaste Mrs Hutton* by John Dempster

Questions

1   What sensational thing would Mr Hutton like to do to his wife?
2   What does he think of doing to himself?
3   What does happen in the end?

You can use **an open ending**, which suggests the outcome of the plot, but leaves the reader to supply the conclusion.

The train gave a great wailing blast of whistle, the porters cried out all along the line, the cars jolted, and his special porter waved and smiled down at the boy there . . . as the whistle screamed again.

'What?' shouted the porter, hand cupped to ear.

'Wish me luck!' cried Willie.

'Best of luck, son,' called the porter, waving, smiling. 'Best of luck, boy!'

'Thanks,' said Willie, in the great sound of the train, in the steam and roar.

He watched the black train until it was completely gone away and out of sight. He did not move all the time it was going. He stood quietly a small boy twelve years old, on the worn wooden platform, and only after three entire minutes did he turn at last to face the empty streets below.

Then, as the sun was rising, he began to walk very fast, so as to keep warm, down into the new town.

from *Hail and Farewell* by Ray Bradbury

Questions

1   What seems to have happened to the boy so far? How is this suggested to you?
2   What questions does the writer leave unanswered?

You can have **an unexpected ending**, by providing a **'twist'** to the story. Read the following story carefully.

The Visitor

David swiftly scribbled the last line of his homework and glanced at the kitchen clock. It was only a quarter to nine, which meant he had about an hour to watch the television, before his parents returned home and sent him to bed. He was about to go into the dining room, when he heard a noise from the lounge. David quietly walked across the hall and cautiously opened the lounge door.

The person, who was standing in the middle of the room, turned round sharply and then looked at David, sheepishly. He was dressed in a long, white, flowing robe and was holding a clipboard.

'I've ... um ... come to read the gas meter,' said the person looking hopefully at David.

'Come off it,' David replied scornfully. The man looked extremely uncomfortable. 'I'm sorry. I know that it wasn't convincing but, it's the best I can contrive at the moment.' The man paused and then continued, 'I mean, you wouldn't believe me, if I said I'm supposed to be collecting an 'A type' soul from this house, at twenty to nine, would you?'

'Are you saying you're an angel?' gasped David, in total disbelief.

The young man nodded,

David scrutinised the 'angel' for a minute or so, and decided to humour him. 'I'm afraid no one's died here lately,' he said casually. 'Are you sure you've got the right date?' The Angel examined his clipboard nervously.

'Well, it is the 15th March, isn't it? I haven't been doing this time-travelling long – I don't think I've quite grasped the idea.'

'Neither do I,' replied David. 'You're a week early!' A look of horror passed over the angel's face.

'Do you realise what this means? I have to go back to the

time when I first arrived here and then tell myself to come back a week later!' David frantically tried to remember what his physics teacher had told him about the theory of time travel.

'Doesn't that mean,' he said, thoughtfully, 'that time will go backward, until it reaches the point when you arrived here and everything after that will cease to exist?'

'Something like that,' replied the angel. 'Anyway I've got to go.' The angel straightened his gown and clasped his clipboard against his chest.

'Hang on a minute,' cried David, 'since I won't remember any of this, whose soul are you going to get?' The angel was in the process of fading away. David asked again and a dim voice answered him, 'David something'.

David had finished his homework and was about to go into the dining room when he heard a voice from the lounge. He walked quietly across the hall, but when he opened the lounge door, there was nobody there.

Angela Darby, aged 15

Questions

1 What twist occurs in the story as the angel is leaving? How does the writer make this so surprising?

2 What is happening in the last paragraph? How good an ending is it to the story?

Read the following few paragraphs of a pupil's narrative essay. Write five different endings to the story in each of the styles described for you.

Attention Great Britain!

The steam from warm fish rose into the stale air of the sitting room. The man carrying the tray which supported his supper, reached out a strong firm hand and pressed the necessary button on the ageing TV set, then began his supper. The brightly coloured picture slowly materialised on the crackling tube and the man groaned.

'Oh hell, not another current affairs programme!'

He moved across his dingy flat room to press the button. The screen fizzed and went blank for a few moments. The picture returned and he was shocked to see the figure of a stern looking woman staring out of the screen at him. She spoke.

'Attention Great Britain! Attention Great Britain! This is a national emergency. I am sorry to inform you that several very powerful guided atomic missiles have been launched from somewhere in the Far East and are at the moment travelling on a pre-set trajectory towards most of the capital cities within the United Kingdom.'

'Jesus Christ!' the man half screamed.

'Unfortunately our defensive systems are incapable of dealing with this type of supersonic missile so it is necessary for every citizen within the Kingdom to make his or her way to the local fallout shelter and await further instructions there. The estimated time of impact is fifteen minutes twenty seconds. Please do not panic but make your way to safety within the specified time period.'

The screen went blank again and the piercing wail of sirens flowed steadily out of the speakers.

Peter Woodhead, aged 16

Approaches to narrative

When you are writing a narrative, be as original as possible. To do this you not only need to write an imaginative story, but must give it **an interesting structure**. It is also important to decide whether to tell the story in the first person or the third.

> You can use the structure of **giving the story a twist** to it. This keeps the reader's interest to the very end. Read the following essay which is written in this way.

The Anniversary

James Swindon was driving along the new dual carriageway which led from central London to the outer suburbs. It was a pleasant evening with little traffic and, as he cruised along in his smart black Jaguar, his concentration began to wander. Occasionally the glare of the setting sun between the leafy trees caught his eyes. He flipped the sun visor down and caught his reflection in the mirror. 'Not bad,' he thought contentedly. At thirty five he was good looking, successful and a moderately wealthy business man.

The road he travelled along twice daily now became monotonous. As he drove along, bleary-eyed, something caught his eye. It was a person standing on the kerb – or was it? Quite awake now, he rubbed his eyes gently and felt the tension in the back of his neck. He sighed deeply. The sun was too bright.

After travelling half a mile, he saw another figure ahead of him. 'Now he is definitely there,' thought James.

The man was standing right on the kerb with his thumb out at his side. 'Hitchhikers make interesting conversation,' said James to himself as he indicated and slowed down beside him. Close up the hitchhiker looked about thirty with a sallow complexion, dark brown hair and a rugged beard. At first sight he appeared quite well-built but James observed that he must have had at least two thick jumpers on. Strange for a mid-July day, James thought. He wound down the window and the man greeted him with a relieved and grateful smile, exposing two rows of perfect white teeth.

'Hello,' James greeted him with a small wave.

'Hi,' the man replied in a very deep, very Scottish voice.

'I'm going to Basildon if that's any help,' said James.

The man's face seemed to shadow over for a few seconds then he said, 'Fine.' James opened the door, the man climbed in throwing his small black backpack on to the seat behind him.

'My name's Billy. Billy McLeod,' said the man gruffly.

'Ah, truly Scottish,' said James, offering him his hand. 'Truly Scottish.' The two men exchanged greetings and James changed gear, quickly moving into the fast lane.

'Well, where are you hoping to go – after Basildon?'

'I'm making my way to Felixstowe and then on to Norwich,' said Billy confidently. He added, 'In search of a lost grandparent. Whether I'll get there I don't know,' he said staring blankly at the road in front of him. James furrowed his brow in wonder at Billy's last statement. He was just about to ask why when Billy started coughing. He produced a handkerchief, wrapped inside it was a pocket watch. It read a quarter past five. 'For safety,' said Billy quickly slipping it into his other pocket. James inconspicuously glanced at his watch. His digital quartz read a quarter past six. It never fails, thought James. Never.

'Have you ever been down here before?' 'Yes!' said Billy, suddenly flashing his teeth. 'Sometime ago. By the way watch this bend up here, many lives have come to an end there. Tragic.' James's adrenalin started flowing. 'But this carriageway's only been built a year.'

There was a sudden silence.

'It's my anniversary today,' said Billy.

'I . . . what . . . what anniversary?' said James confused.

'The anniversary,' he paused, 'of my death on this bend at a quarter past five one year ago.'

At that moment, all that James heard was a gruff laughing as the petrol tanker careered around the bend.

Ann Woodhead, aged 15

Questions

1 What atmosphere is created at the beginning of the story?
2 When does the atmosphere change? Explain why.
3 What does James find surprising about the hitchhiker's appearance and what he says?
4 What is the anniversary? What is the twist to the story?
5 Why do you think the writer has chosen to tell the story in the third person?

You can use **a flashback**. In this technique, the ending of the story forms the first paragraph. Then the narrator describes the events which have led up to this end, by means of memories or 'flashbacks'.

The Loss

The gentle power of the giant's limbs was all too apparent to me as I stood, tear-stained, hands thrust defiantly in my pockets, watching the executioners prepare their deadly scaffold. My tousled hair blew erratically in the angry wind keeping in time with the last proud movements of the leaves on the old oak that towered before me. I sniffed despairingly and watched as the oak, my guardian, my protector, was advanced upon by the workmen and their tools of death and destruction.

My mind recalled with pleasure the security derived from the oak over the last three of my six years. I vividly pictured the times when I had sat brooding in the cool embrace of its shadow, and emerged from its touch in a clearer frame of mind. My delight at the boundless reach of the old oak's limbs was beyond compare and rivalled only by my awe for the tree's strength and stability. The past winds, rains and snow had made little headway against the power of that mighty giant, and this I recognised and respected, and whilst others played on the swings, here I would sit.

I remembered especially my first school day, of the torture derived from those hours of tedious ritual and of my relief when freed from its chains. On that night I had come to the folds of the tree and sunk into its comforting grip. On that night I had again received its soothing influence, and my moodiness and anger at my unwilling entry into school life had been dispersed. I emerged in a more determined mind to attack my school work in the way that my parents wished. For that, I thanked the great oak.

It had been a bright Saturday when I left my mother for the comfort of the tree only to see it in an embrace it could not escape; that of men and their machines. I had stayed long enough to be certain of their intentions, before fleeing in tortured panic to seek the solace and companionship of my mother in my time of trouble. She tried desperately to help me but to no avail. It was as a parting gesture and a show of my gratitude, that I had come to comfort the tree in its final hour of freedom.

Now, as I watched those powerful limbs fall to the harsh cold ground, and the trunk of the tree being hacked down, my defiance melted and tears flowed freely across my stricken face. Finally, as the great oak proved its mere mortality and was allowed to fall unceremoniously to the awaiting clutches of the ground from which it had sprung, I let out a last sob and looked for solitude, elsewhere ......

Ian Cade, aged 15

Questions

1 The first paragraph deals with the climax of the story. What is it?
2 What do the 'flashbacks' tell you about the importance of the tree to the narrator?
3 How does the story benefit from being told in the first person?

You can write a story which **makes a comment on human behaviour.**

The Lesson

Giggling, screaming, the three girls careered into the play-room of Mrs Roeburn's pre-school nursery. They descended upon this gracious lady like a flock of hungry gannets, demanding 'The Dolls'.

'Yes, darlings, you shall have them right away.'

'Miss, there's some new 'uns.'

'Yes, dear, aren't they sweet? Now run along and play, there's a good little poppet.'

The good little poppets ran along, clutching their new acquisitions tightly to their skimpy little chests.

'She said the new 'uns were sweet. But they're not.' Polly was indignant. 'No. I hates 'em.'

Lucy was indiscreet enough to enquire why. Polly and Jenny came down upon her from the pinnacle afforded them by dint of their superior knowledge.

'Well dear, just look at the colour.'

'That sort, you know, they shouldn't be allowed.'

'Oh!' Enlightenment smacked her sharply. 'You mean . . .'

'Well,' Polly was in her element. 'Something has to be done about it.'

The three sat and silently observed the new dolls. Flesh and blood staring down; rubber and plastic staring up. Pink skin; brown plastic. Hair blond and straight; black and wiry. Eyes blue and cold; brown and hard.

Suddenly the three pounced. The New Dolls were dismembered. Eyes were wrenched out, skin was scratched and torn, hair was tossed in bunches across the playroom. The three beat, crushed, kicked. The dolls were beaten, crushed, kicked.

Satisfied they made a little heap of the carnage, then sat back and surveyed it. Gratification and realisation swept over them.

'Mrs Roeburn, we've had *such* a lovely game.'

Audrey MacDonald, aged 14

1 In your own words, sum up the plot of this story.
2 What two points does the writer use the story to illustrate?
3 Why has the writer used so much direct speech in this narrative?

You can use a **recurring idea** to link each stage in the development of a story, as this essay shows.

The Storm

She had nursed him all day long through fever and delirium and now as dusk began to fall she felt exhausted. In the distance she could hear the faint rumblings of a storm and felt glad. Perhaps now the air would be clearer: it would be cooler and maybe his illness would not be so bad.

As night closed in, his condition got more severe. As the storm grew louder his fever grew worse. If only he had not saved those children from the fire in the old mill. They had been there for days and were riddled with typhoid. He had brought them home and nursed them but to no avail, and they had died. Now he had got the fever himself and she prayed that he was not going to die too.

The storm grew to a crescendo and he screamed out in pain. The lightning flashed and the thunder reverberated around the house, but suddenly as quickly as the storm had appeared it subsided.

As the storm rumbled away he seemed to pick up and gradually the fever abated. She stood up and went to make some gruel. She turned and saw him watching her.

'Mary,' he croaked.

Suddenly the sun seemed to be shining as she realised he was going to be alright.

Michaela Jones, aged 16

Questions

1 In your own words, explain the story being told in this essay.
2 What are the important stages of the story?
3 How does the writer use the storm to show these stages?

Practice work   Here is a plan for a narrative essay about a young girl, who has lost someone dear to her.

THE CHURCHYARD

Girl enters. Watches vicar and congregation leave church. Sad. Breeze wafts smell of freshly cut grass and flowers. Looks at them.

THE FLOWERS

Colours bright, happy. Delicate fragile petals. Wind blows petals. Notices brown fading edges. Signs of Autumn approaching.

MOVES TOWARDS GRAVEYARD

Moves slowly. Attention caught by violets. Remembers memory of another occasion when flowers seen in summer. Happy then but now... Stamps on flowers viciously. Why should they live?

REACHES GRAVE

'To the memory of...' Bunch of withered flowers in vase. Illegally picked from under tree last time. Looks at spot – new flowers there! Death of old ones brings birth of new!

---

1   Why is the main character in the story in the churchyard?
2   What is the 'memory' she has of her past?
3   How do her thoughts and feelings change?
4   Why do these changes occur, and how are they shown?
5   What is the recurring idea which links the stages of the story?

Using the information in the plan, and the answers to these questions, develop the ideas for each paragraph. Write the essay you have planned out.

Essay work   Write one of the following essays **using the skills** you have learned. This means deciding on the time, setting, characters and plot. The story needs to be planned out, and a suitable introduction and conclusion chosen. **Remember to work from a rough draft to a final version.**

1   Choose one of the following and continue the story.

a)   It's a long story and it took some time to happen; and it began a good many years ago, in October as well as I can remember.

b)   One o'clock on Saturday afternoon.
Suddenly the sirens began. Their sound swooped into the basement kitchen at 46 Marling Street, Camden Town . . .

c)   He finished stopping up the cracks of the bedroom window with the putty knife and the scraps of dirty rag. Outside it was already snowing, in sharp wind-scurried bursts, with particles of ice that bounced like grains of rice on the black dry pavements.

2   Write a story on one of the following:
The Gift
The Silence
The Broken Appointment

3   Write a short story which illustrates one of the following:
Intolerance
Pride
Jealousy
Meanness
Patience

Picture   4   Look at the picture and write the story it suggests to you.

2 Descriptive writing

When you are describing an event or a place you must have a specific scene in mind, so that you can 'paint a picture in words'. To do this you need to give a detailed account of a scene. You can organise your ideas by using your senses. It is also important to suggest the special qualities an event or place has, by describing its atmosphere. Make your description vivid by choosing words with care, and by using comparisons (**similes** and **metaphors**) imaginatively and appropriately.

Giving the details

Here are two passages which describe the French town of Avignon. Read them carefully and answer the questions which follow.

Avignon

1

Avignon is a French town in Provence, on the Rhône, and is the capital of the département of Vaucluse. Although dating from Roman times it did not rise in importance until the Middle Ages. In 1226 it was besieged by Louis VIII during the crusade against the Albigensian Movement. From 1309 until 1388, Avignon was the residence of the Popes and the prosperity of the town dates from this time. The French anti-Popes used Avignon as their seat (1378–1408). The high, crenellated ramparts, dating from the fourteenth century, still exist; on the north side is the Rocher des Doms, now a public garden, rising steeply from the river. The famous twelfth-century Saint Bénézet bridge, immortalised in the folk song 'Sur le Pont D'Avignon' has been in ruins since 1669. It is flanked by a Romanesque chapel (1234 – 1237). The archiepiscopal cathedral stands beside the enormous fortress palace of the popes, one of the most magnificent Gothic buildings of the fourteenth century. The town is much visited by tourists.

from *Everyman Encyclopaedia*

2

Avignon is a walled city, as I have said, a compact and lovely little town skirted to the north and west by the Rhône and circled completely by medieval ramparts, none the less lovely, to my inexpert eye, for having been heavily restored in the nineteenth century. The city is dominated from the north by the Rocher des Doms, a steep mass of white rock crowned by the cathedral of Notre Dame, and green with singing pines. Beside the cathedral, taking the light above the town is the golden stone palace of the

Popes. The town itself is slashed in two by one main street, the Rue de la République, which leads from the main gate straight up to the city square and thence to the Place du Palais, at the foot of Rocher des Doms itself.

But these things I had yet to find. It was dusk when I set out, and the street was vividly lit. All the cafés were full and I picked my way between the tables on the pavement, where there grew in me that slow sense of exhilaration which one inevitably gets in a Southern town after dark. The shop windows glittered and flashed with every conceivable luxury that the mind of the tourist could imagine, the neon lights slid along satin and drowned themselves in velvet and danced over perfumed jewels, and, since I have learned in my 28 years to protect the heart a little against too much pity, I kept my eyes on them, and tried not to think about the beggars who slunk whining along the city gutters. I went on, carefully not thinking about those beggars, until I reached the end of the street, where the Rue de la République widens out and becomes the main square of the city and where all Avignon collects at night, together with one would swear every child and every dog in France.

The square is surrounded with cafés, which overflow the narrow pavements with a froth of gay little tables and wicker chairs, and even cast up a jetsam of more little tables across the roads and into the centre of the square itself. There, as I said, Avignon collects at night, and for the price of a cup of coffee which secures you a chair, you may sit for an hour and watch France parade for you.

This time I went out of the city gate, and turned along under the massive outer walls, towards the quarter where the Rhône races under the Rocher des Doms and then around the western fortifications of the city. But presently, round a curve in the city wall, the old bridge of the song came into view, its four remaining arches soaring out across the green water to break off, as it were in mid leap, suspended half-way across the Rhône. Down into the deep jade water glimmered the drowned golden reflection of the chapel of St Nicholas, which guards the second arch.

from *Madam Will You Talk?* by Mary Stewart

Questions

1 What detailed information about Avignon is given in both passages?

2 Explain how the words on page 40 in **bold** type, taken from the second passage, give a more vivid impression of the appearance of the town than those used by the first writer. Refer back to the first passage to justify your comments.

Example

'A compact and lovely town **skirted to the north and west by the Rhône** and **circled completely by medieval ramparts**'

The first passage just says that Avignon is on the Rhône, and that the town has crenellated ramparts. In this phrase the impression given is that Avignon is an attractive place. 'Skirted' explains that the Rhône touches the outer limits of the town on the north and west. 'Circled by medieval ramparts' makes Avignon seem an historical and rather enclosed place. This description is more specific than that in the first passage, and the details make it easier to visualise the position of the town.

Try to express your ideas in the same detailed way.

'The city is **dominated** from the north by the Rocher des Doms, **a steep mass of white rock crowned by the cathedral** of Notre Dame, and green with **singing** pines.'

'**taking the light above the town is the golden stone** palace of the Popes'

'The town itself is **slashed in two by one main street**'

'the old bridge of the song came into view, its four remaining arches **soaring out across the green water to break off, as it were in mid leap**'

'Down into the **deep jade water glimmered the drowned golden reflection** of the chapel of St Nicholas'

3   What kind of detailed information is given only in the first passage? What does it add to the description of the town?

4   The second passage includes the following details about Avignon which are not mentioned by the writer of the first passage. Explain what each one adds to the impression created of the town. Refer to specific words and phrases to justify your views.

'The shop windows glittered and flashed with every conceivable luxury the mind of the tourist could imagine, the neon lights slid along satin and drowned themselves in velvet and danced over perfumed jewels.'

'The square is surrounded with cafés, which overflow the narrow pavements with a froth of gay little tables and wicker chairs, and even cast up a jetsam of more little tables across the roads.'

Practice work

1   Here are some sentences which were written as first drafts. Using the basic details given in each sentence, rewrite them to make the description as vivid as possible.
An example has been done for you.

Example

Before us the outline of the house's roof and chimneys could be seen against the night sky.

Before us lay the <u>dark bulk</u> of the house, its serrated roof and bristling chimneys hard outlined against the <u>silver-spangled sky</u>.

- There was light in the lower window of the house, which shone on the orchard and the moor.

- The red bricks of the town's buildings were grimy with smoke.

- The early morning sun shone on the weather vane as it moved in the breeze, and then shone on the rest of the grey house.

- The shutters on the house were closed, and there was ivy on the walls.

- It was sunset, and the light shone on the sea and cliffs.

- In the town centre, the shops were brightly lit and loud music could be heard coming from them.

Picture

2   Look at the pictures overleaf carefully. Write a paragraph to describe each scene vividly.

3   Choose a village, town or city which you know well, and write a detailed factual description of it. Using the same basic information, write another description of the chosen place, in such a way as to bring it to life, by 'painting a picture in words'.

Using the senses

A good way to gather ideas for a descriptive essay is to use the senses. Organise your ideas under what you can see, hear, smell, taste and feel. This will give your essay a structure.

> In this extract, Dylan Thomas describes a day he spent at the seaside when he was a child. He has a specific outing in mind, which took place one August Bank Holiday. Read the passage carefully.

The Seaside

And the trams that hissed like ganders took us all to the beautiful beach.

There was cricket on the sand, and sand in the sponge cake, sandflies in the watercress, and foolish, mulish, religious donkeys on the unwilling trot. Girls undressed in slipping tents of propriety; under invisible umbrellas, stout ladies dressed for the male and immoral sea. Little naked navvies dug canals; children with spades and no ambition built fleeting castles; wispy young men outside bathing huts whistled at substantial young women and dogs who desired thrown stones more than the bones of elephants. Recalcitrant uncles huddled over luke ale in the tiger-striped marquees. Mothers in black, like wobbling mountains, gasped under the discarded dresses of daughters who shrilly braved the goblin waves. And fathers, in the once-a-year sun, took fifty winks, Oh, think of all the fifty winks along the paper-bagged sand.

Liquorice allsorts, and Welsh hearts, were melting, and the sticks of rock, that we all sucked, were like barbers' poles made of rhubarb.

In the distance, surrounded by disappointed theoreticians and an ironmonger with a drum, a cross man on an orange-box shouted that holidays were wrong.

And the waves rolled in, with rubber ducks and clerks upon them.

I remember the patient, laborious, and enamouring hobby, or profession, of burying relatives in sand.

I remember the princely pastime of pouring sand, from cupped hands or buckets, down collars and tops of dresses; the shriek, the shake, the slap.

I can remember the boy by himself, the beachcombing lone-wolf, hungrily waiting at the edge of family cricket; the friendless fielder, the boy uninvited to bat or to tea.

I remember the smell of sea and seaweed, wet flesh, wet hair, wet bathing dresses, the warm smell as of a rabbity field after rain, the smell of pop and splashed sunshades and toffee, the stable-and-straw smell of hot, tossed, tumbled, dug and trodden sand, the swill-and-gaslamp smell of Saturday night, though the sun shone strong, from the bellying beer-tents, the smell of the vinegar on shelled cockles, winkle smell, shrimp smell, the dripping-oily backstreet winter smell of chips in newspapers, the smell of ships from the sun-dazed docks round the corner of the sand hills, the smell of the known and paddled-in sea moving full of the drowned and herrings, out and away beyond and further still towards the antipodes that hung their koala bears and Maoris, kangaroos and boomerangs, upside down over the backs of the stars.

And the noise of pummelling Punch and Judy falling, and a clock tolling or telling no time in the tenantless town; now and again a bell from a lost tower or a train on the lines behind us clearing its throat, and always the hopeless, ravenous swearing and pleading of the gulls, donkey bray and hawker cry, harmonicas and toy trumpets, shouting and laughing and singing, hooting of tugs and tramps, the clip of the chair attendant's puncher, the motorboat coughing in the bay, and the same hymn and washing of the sea that was heard in the Bible.

from *Holiday Memory* by Dylan Thomas

Questions

1 What does Dylan Thomas remember seeing during his day at the seaside?

2 What sounds was he aware of?

3 What smells and tastes did he experience?

4 What did he experience through his sense of touch?

5 Explain what impression the writer creates by his imaginative use of words in each of the following. Pay particular attention to the bold words.

'and **foolish, mulish, religious donkeys** on the unwilling trot'

'children with spades and **no ambition built fleeting castles**'

'and always the **hopeless, ravenous swearing and pleading** of the gulls'

'And the trams **that hissed like ganders**'

'Little naked **navvies dug canals**'

'**Recalcitrant** uncles **huddled** over luke ale in the **tiger-striped marquees.**'

'Mothers in black, **like wobbling mountains**, gasped'

'and the sticks of rock, that we all sucked, **were like barbers' poles made of rhubarb**'

'from the **bellying** beer-tents'

'the motorboat **coughing** in the bay'

6 Choose five examples of other words or phrases, which you consider to be used imaginatively, and explain why you have chosen them.

Practice work

Picture

Look at the picture carefully. Make a list of words and phrases connected with what you can see, hear, smell, taste and feel. You may find it useful to draw up four columns as shown here.

What can I see?	What can I hear?	What can I smell/taste?	What can I feel?

Essay work

Write an essay describing the scene using the ideas you have collected.

Suggesting the atmosphere

Here the writer has given a detailed description of a place by using her senses. She shows how the place affected her, and suggests its atmosphere.

The Amusement Arcade

It was here that a few amusements were situated. Most of them were closed at this time of year, but I liked to wander past the canvas shrouded dodgem cars and shuttered gift stalls. I enjoyed the tawdriness of it all, the blank lights and peeling paint. There was an open air swimming pool, drained for the winter, and sand and silt had been washed over the rim by the storm tides. Near to this was a café and one amusement centre, called Gala Land, both of which remained open.

I could not keep away from Gala Land. It had a particular smell which drew me down the steep flight of concrete steps to the pay desk below. It was built underground in a sort of valley between two outcrops of rock, over which was a ribbed glass roof, like those of Victorian railway stations and conservatories. The walls were covered in greenish moss and the whole place had a close, damp, musty smell and although it was lit from end to end with neon and fluorescent lights, everything looked somehow dark, furtive and gone to seed. Some of the booths were closed down here, too, and those which kept open must have lost money, except perhaps on the few days when parties of trippers came from inland, in the teeth of the weather, and dived down for shelter to the underground fun palace. Then, for a few hours, the fruit and try-your-strength and fortune card machines whirred, loud cracks echoed from the rifle ranges, hurdygurdy music sounded out, there was a show of gaiety. For the rest of the time the place was mainly patronised by a few unemployed men and teenage boys, who chewed gum and fired endless rounds of blank ammunition at the bobbing rows of duck targets, and by older school children after four o'clock. At the far end was a roller skating rink which drew a good crowd on Saturday afternoons.

I liked the sad, shabby place, I liked its atmosphere. Occasionally I put a coin into a fruit machine or watched 'What the Butler Saw'. There was a more gruesome peep-show, too, in which one could watch a condemned man being led on to a platform, hooded and noosed and then dropped snap, down through a trapdoor to death. I watched this so often, that, long after I had left the town, this scene featured in my nightmares, I smelled the brackish, underground smell.

from *Mr Proudham and Mr Sleight* by Susan Hill

Questions

1 In the first paragraph, how does the description of what the writer can see suggest the amusements were dull and lifeless?
2 What is suggested by the use of the metaphor 'canvas shrouded dodgem cars'? How is this idea supported by the description of the location of Gala Land in the second paragraph?
3 How does the smell contribute to the impression of Gala Land?
4 What is meant by 'everything looked dark, furtive and gone to seed'? List the things described from that point to the end of the extract which might give this impression.
5 How does the writer suggest Gala Land's magnetic quality?

> It is possible for a place to have different atmospheres according to circumstances, as the following extracts show.

The Old House

1

At last the shutters and doors were closed. In silence and in darkness stood the magnificent old house. The moon rose full and high generously shedding light which quenched the blackness, bathed the house in silver and gave an air of enchantment. The silver pall was amplified by the rich backdrop of the evening sky. Only the occasional solitary cloud glided by to cast a shadow on the scene. The marble steps, leading to the sweeping lawns, were softened in the pallid glow. The walkway, strewn with fine white quartz, glinted and flickered with life. The now illuminated statues glowed with form and texture. Shrubs on the walk and lawns were set in stark relief, as beams of light played on their delicate yet luxuriant foliage. Lush velvet grass rippled in the gentle breeze. Dark silhouettes of forest trees towered majestically over the setting, only bending occasionally in the whispering breeze. The deep-throated, gentle hooting of the owl only served to accentuate the tranquillity. Something moved imperceptibly in the shadows . . . . . .

2

With shutters and doors closed, the dark rambling house stood in ominous silence. The moon rose full and high, and the unearthly white light swamped the house revealing its stark grimness. The ghostly sphere stood out against the hellish blackness of the night sky. Creeping shadows were formed by funereal clouds. The marble steps were frozen cold and harsh in the intense pallor. Many statues loomed up like weird phantoms on the walkway which was strewn with icy sharp quartz. The shrubs drained of their natural colour, glowed pale and menacing in the darkness. The grass moved with mysterious life. Dark silhouettes of the forest trees oppressed the scene. They spoke in mournful tones as they moved like spectres in the wind. The soulless hooting of the owl momentarily pierced the air; uncanny silence followed. Something moved imperceptibly in the shadows . . . . . .

Questions

1   What atmosphere is created in each of these passages?
2   How does the description of the moonlight on the house, the walkway and the grounds create the atmosphere in each passage?
3   What sort of stories would each of these passages introduce?

Practice work   Draw up five columns as shown here.

What can I see?	What can I hear?	What can I smell/taste?	What can I feel?	What is the atmosphere?

Picture   Look at the picture. Make a list of words and phrases connected with what you can see, hear, smell, taste and feel in the appropriate columns. Jot down some words which suggest the atmosphere of the scene. Write two descriptions of the scenes suggesting a different atmosphere in each case.

Here is a **rough draft** of an essay.

The drive was narrow and twisting and there were trees on either side. The trees were thick and did not let in much light so it was dark. It was very quiet and very stuffy after the breeze on the road. Even the car engine did not sound as loud as it had done on the high road. The drive went downhill and there were lots more trees. We went on over a bridge and the path still twisted and turned and the trees got thicker and thicker and it got quieter. I felt very frightened as we did not seem to be getting anywhere near the house. I began to panic and wished we would hurry up and reach the end of the drive. Then the trees began to clear and I could see the sky and suddenly there were lots of bright red rhododendron bushes. They were lovely and there were masses of them. They made a change from the darkness of the wood. Then the house appeared. It was even nicer than I had expected and had lots of lawns and gardens that went down to the sea.

Develop it into an essay describing the journey through the estate to the house. Use the basic ideas provided in the passage but develop them to give detailed descriptions of the grounds and the house. Decide on the atmosphere you wish to create and make it clear throughout.

51

Using adjectives and comparisons

Adjectives and comparisons are particularly useful in creating a vivid impression of a scene. In this extract the writer describes a visit to an Austrian circus. Read it carefully and answer the questions which follow.

The Circus

A dwarf in a scarlet baggy costume sold us our programme and ushered us into our chairs. The tent was filled with music from some vast amplifier: as always in Austria, the music was pleasant: even in a small village circus we were expected to listen to Offenbach and Suppé and Strauss. The tent was not a big one, but the floodlights on the poles of the four 'corners' of the ring threw so much brilliance down into the ring that above them the top of the tent seemed a vast floating darkness, and very high. Caught by a flicker of light the high wire glittered like thread. On their platforms near the tops of the poles the electricians crouched behind their lights, waiting. There was the circus smell which is a mingling of sharp animal sweat and trampled grass, and with this the curiously pungent smell of continental tobacco. The big lights moved, the music changed, and a march blared out. The curtains at the back of the ring were pulled open, and the procession began.

For a small circus, the standard of performance was remarkably good. Herr Wagner himself was the ringmaster, a short stocky man, who even in the frock coat and top hat of his calling, looked every inch a horseman. The 'rodeo' which followed the procession, was an exciting stampede of horses – real old-fashioned 'circus' horses, piebald and dun-coloured and spotted – supported a wild-act with some clever rope work and voltige riding. Annalisa appeared only briefly, barely recognisable as a cowgirl eclipsed by a ten-gallon hat, and riding a hideous spotted horse with a pink muzzle and pink rimmed eyes, which looked as clumsy as a hippo, and was as clever on its feet as the Maltese cat. Then came a comic act with a donkey, and after it Herr

Wagner again, with his liberty horses. These were beautiful, every one a star, ten well-matched palaminos with coats the colour of wild silk, and manes and tails of creamy floss. They wheeled in under the lights, plumes tossing, silk manes flying, breaking and performing their circles, rearing one after the other in line, so that the plumes and the floss-silk manes tossed up like the crest of a breaking wave. Rods and shafts of lime-light, falling from above moved and criss-crossed in patterns of golden-light, following the golden horses. Light ran and glittered on them. They were sun horses, bridled and plumed with gold, obedient you would have sworn to the pull of those rods of light, as the white horses of the wavecrests are to the pull of the moon. Then the tossing plumes subsided, the flying hoofs met the ground again, the music stopped and they were just ten self-satisfied horses, queueing at Herr Wagner's pockets for sugar.

The trumpets brayed and the ringmaster made his announcement, the red curtain parted, and a white horse broke from the shadows behind the ring and cantered into the lime-light. On his back, looking prettier than ever, screne and competent and tough as a whiplash in a dark blue version of a hussar's uniform, was Annalisa. The horse was not plumed and harnessed as the liberty horses had been; he was dressed for business, but the bridle was a magnificent affair of scarlet studded with gold, and his saddlecloth glittered and flashed with colours as if every jewel that had ever been discovered was stitched into its silk.

from *Airs Above the Ground* by Mary Stewart

Questions

1 What did the people see as they entered the circus? Why was the scene so vivid?
2 Explain what impression is created of the circus acts by the adjectives and comparisons in the following.

'The 'rodeo' which followed the procession, was an exciting stampede of horses – real old-fashioned 'circus' horses, piebald and dun-coloured and spotted'

'Annalisa appeared only briefly, barely recognisable as a cowgirl eclipsed by a ten-gallon hat'

'riding a hideous spotted horse with a pink muzzle and pink rimmed eyes, which looked as clumsy as a hippo, and was as clever on its feet as the Maltese cat'

'ten well-matched palaminos with coats the colour of wild silk, and manes and tails of creamy floss'

'They wheeled in under the lights, plumes tossing, silk manes flying'

'the plumes and the floss-silk manes tossed up like the crest of a breaking wave'

3   What effect did the lighting have on the appearance of the liberty horses?

4   Make a list of the adjectives used in the description of Annalisa's final act. What impression of the scene do they create?

Ruth's husband, Joe, has died in tragic circumstances. As Ruth remains alone in their cottage wishing time away, she observes the changing seasons.

Journey through the Year

Winter
The woods and coppices were still leafless, branches open-meshed, or else pointing up, thin and dark against the blue-white sky; she could see all the way down between the wide-spaced beech trunks, to the fields below.

Spring
All the colours of the day were green and gold, even the sky seemed to have taken on the reflection from the white-gold sun and the upturned petals of yellow flowers in field and meadow, and along the margins of the wood.

As they stood at the top of the field for a moment, looking down, Ruth saw, first, the haze of green, like an open-work shawl laid over the tops of the trees, where the buds were unfolding into first leaf. Ruth thought she could never have seen so many shades of green; the emerald of the larches that fringed the beech woods, and the yellowish-green early poplars, ash-green willow leaves and the pale, oaten-olive tinge of the young wheat. The grass was green, dark as moss in the shadows of the banks, and clear as lime, high up in the full sun, and when they went into the wood, the light was pond-green and, at their feet, the polished green blades of bluebells.

There were lemon primroses, and the deeper tinted cowslips, celandines and rich marsh marigolds, the last of the miniature daffodils, and dandelions, bright as medallions – which might be weeds but were beautiful enough for any grave.

Summer

It was June. Hot. But the trees were still a fresh sappy green, and the hay was full of clover. Traveller's joy and the white, bell flowers of convolvulus were thrown over all the hedges and trailed down like ragged clothes set out to dry, the fields were set about with ox-eye daisies and corn marigolds. Every day, Ruth picked handfuls of different flowers, white and mauve and butter yellow . . . . . .

Autumn

. . . . . . Summer slipped into the beginning of autumn, as a hand into a familiar glove. She smelled it first of all, going out of the back door that morning . . . smelled autumn in the fine mist, which had condensed and fallen and lay as a heavy dew, though a few minutes later, the sun was shafting through, drying out the grass again . . . And so much of the world was green and yellow again, but tarnished and dried out, they were not the fresh sappy colours of spring . . . She did not want autumn and winter, and the turning of the year. Yet it would be beautiful; the bracken would gradually shrivel and shrink and curl back within itself and yellow would flare up into orange and burn down again, to a darker brown, and the beech woods would change like the colours of tobacco being slowly, slowly cured. . . . The trees darkened to rust and brown, or paled to topaz yellow, though some lingered, a dull green. Hips and haws reddened in the hedgerows, and on the common and along the lanes the blackberries ripened slowly to the colour of wine, and sloes to slate and indigo blue.

from *In the Spring Time of the Year* by Susan Hill

Questions

1   Draw up four columns like this. In the appropriate column list the adjectives Susan Hill uses to describe the shades of colour to be seen in each of the seasons.

WINTER	SPRING	SUMMER	AUTUMN

2   Explain what impression is being created in each of the following comparisons.

'branches open-meshed'

'the haze of green, like an openwork shawl laid over the tops of the trees'

'the last of the miniature daffodils, and dandelions, bright as medallions'

'bell flowers of convolvulus were thrown over all the hedges and trailed down like ragged clothes set out to dry'

'Summer slipped into the beginning of autumn as a hand into a familiar glove.'

'so much of the world was green and yellow again, but tarnished'

'and yellow would flare up into orange and burn down again'

'the beech woods would change like the colour of tobacco being slowly, slowly cured'

Practice work

Picture

Look at the following picture carefully. Write a vivid description of the scene, paying particular attention to adjectives and comparisons.

Using verbs, adverbs and sentence structure

In the description of movement or action, the choice of verbs and adverbs is of particular importance. They need to be chosen with care so that vague comments about movement are avoided and actions are clearly and precisely described. Sentence structure can also be used to help emphasise the actions taking place.

Read the following extract carefully and answer the questions which follow. A group of students have dug a hole in the road during a rain storm, in order to trap the school bus.

Sabotage

We flattened ourselves completely and peered through the low bushes.

The bus rattled up the road, though not as quickly as we had hoped. It rolled cautiously through a wide puddle some twenty feet ahead; then, seeming to grow bolder as it approached our man-made lake, it speeded up, spraying the water in high sheets of backward waterfalls into the forest. We could hear the students squealing with delight. But instead of the graceful glide through the puddle that its occupants were expecting, the bus emitted a tremendous crack and careened drunkenly into our trap. For a moment it swayed and we held our breath, afraid that it would topple over. Then it sputtered a last murmuring protest and died, its left front wheel in our ditch, its right wheel in the gully, like a lopsided billy goat on its knees.

We covered our mouths and shook with silent laughter.

As the dismayed driver opened the rear emergency exit, the rain poured down upon him in sharp-needled darts. He stood in the doorway looking down with disbelief at his sunken charge; then holding on to the bus, he poked one foot into the water until it was on solid ground before gingerly stepping down. He looked under the bus. He looked at the steaming hood. He looked at the water. Then he scratched his head and cursed.

from *Roll of Thunder, Hear My Cry* by Mildred D. Taylor

Questions

1   The writer is very specific about the movements of the bus during the accident. Make a list of the verbs and adverbs used to describe how the bus moves. Explain how effective you find them in describing the actions taking place.

2   Which words describe the actions of the bus driver?
    What do they show about him?

3   Explain the following comparisons and say how effective you find them in describing what is happening.

    'spraying the water **in high sheets of backward waterfalls** into the forest'

    'the bus emitted a tremendous crack and **careened drunkenly** into our trap'

    'it sputtered a **last murmuring protest and died**'

    'like a lopsided billy goat on its knees'

    'the rain poured down upon him in **sharp-needled darts'**

4   Look at the following sentence carefully.

    'It rolled cautiously through a wide puddle some twenty feet ahead; then, seeming to grow bolder as it approached our man-made lake, it speeded up, spraying the water in high sheets of backward waterfalls into the forest.'

    What does the writer achieve by punctuating it as she does?

5   The bus driver's actions when he got out of the bus could have been described like this:

    He looked under the bus, at the steaming hood and water, then scratched his head and cursed.

    What effect does the writer achieve by punctuating it as she does?

Practice work   A wide vocabulary helps to make descriptive writing interesting.

1   Make a list of verbs and adverbs which describe:
quick movements
slow movements
smooth movements
jerky movements.

2   Here are some sentences which were written as first drafts. The verbs are dull, repetitive and unspecific about the actions being described. Using the basic information, rewrite the sentences in a more interesting way. Use verbs and adverbs from the lists you have already made.

- It was time to escape, so he opened the door, went outside and walked away from the house.
- Since she was angry, she got out of the chair, walked out of the room and closed the door behind her.
- The barking dog came towards the postman who put down his bag, turned round and made his way to the garden gate.
- The high speed train came towards the station, passed through it and went into the tunnel without stopping.
- The horse was frightened by the noise, so it lifted itself up on its hind legs then went off across the field, over the gate and into the lane.

Pictures   Look at the pictures carefully. Using verbs, adverbs, sentence structure and comparisons effectively, write a paragraph describing each of the situations. Use words from your lists.

In this extract, Claudius describes a fight between two gladiators.

The Rabbit Blow

My sympathies were with the soldier, who came into the arena looking very white and shaky – he had been in prison for some days, and the strong light bothered him. But his entire company, who it appeared sympathised very much with him, for the captain was a bully and a beast, shouted in unison for him to pull himself together and defend the company's honour. He straightened up and shouted, 'I'll do my best lads!' His camp nickname, as it happened was 'Roach', and this was enough to put the greater part of the audience on his side, though the guards were pretty unpopular in the city. If a roach were to kill a fisherman that would be a good joke. To have the amphitheatre on one's side is half the battle to a man fighting for his life. The Thessalian, a wiry, long-armed, long-legged fellow, came swaggering in close to him, dressed only in a leather tunic and a hard round cap. He was in good humour, cracking jokes with the front-benches, for his opponent was an amateur, and Livia was paying him a thousand gold pieces for the afternoon if he killed his man after a good fight. They came together in front of the Box and saluted first Augustus, and Livia and then Germanicus and me as joint-presidents, with the usual formula: 'Greetings, sirs. We salute you in Death's Shadow!' We returned the greetings with a formal gesture, but Germanicus said to Augustus: 'Why sir, that chaser's one of my father's veterans. I know him well. He won a crown in Germany for being the first man over an enemy stockade.' Augustus was interested. 'Good,' he said, 'this should be a good fight, then. But in that case the net-man must be ten years younger, and years count in this game.' Then Germanicus signalled for the trumpets to sound and the fight began.

Roach stood his ground, while the Thessalian danced around him. Roach was not such a fool as to waste his strength running after his lightly armed opponent or yet be paralysed into immobility. The Thessalian tried to make him lose his temper by taunting him, but Roach was not to be drawn. Only once did he show any readiness to take the offensive, and the quickness of the thrust drew a roar of delight from the benches. But the Thessalian was away in time. Soon the fight became more lively. The Thessalian made stabs, high and low, with his long trident, which Roach parried easily, but with an eye on the net weighted with small lead pellets, which the Thessalian managed with his left hand.

'Beautiful work!' I heard Livia say to Augustus. 'The best net-man in Rome. He's playing with the soldier. Did you see that? He could have entangled him and got his stroke in then if he had wished. But he's spinning out the fight.'

'Yes,' said Augustus. 'I'm afraid the soldier is done for. He should have kept off drink.'

Augustus had hardly spoken when Roach knocked up the trident and jumped forward, ripping the Thessalian's leather tunic between arm and body. The Thessalian was away in a flash and as he ran he swung the net across Roach's face. By ill-luck a pellet struck Roach in the eye, momentarily blinding him. He checked his pace and the Thessalian, seeing his advantage, turned and knocked the sword spinning out of his hand. Roach sprang to retrieve it but the Thessalian got there first, ran with it to the barrier and tossed it to a rich patron sitting in the front rank reserved for knights. Then he returned to the pleasant task of goading and despatching an unarmed man. The net whistled round Roach's head and the trident jabbed here and there; but Roach was still undismayed, and once made a snatch at the trident and nearly got possession of it. The Thessalian had now worked himself towards our Box to make a spectacular killing.

'That's enough!' said Livia in a matter-of-fact voice. 'He's done enough playing about. He ought to finish him now.' The Thessalian needed no prompting. He made a simultaneous sweep of his net around Roach's head and a stab at his belly with the trident. And then what a roar went up! Roach had caught the net with his right hand, and, flinging his body back, kicked with all his strength at the staff of the trident a foot or two from his enemy's hand. The weapon flew up over the Thessalian's head, turned in the air and struck quivering into the wooden barrier. The Thessalian stood astonished for a moment, then felt the net in Roach's hand and dashed past him to recover the trident. Roach threw himself forward and sideways and caught him in the ribs, as he ran, with the spiked boss of his shield. The Thessalian fell, gasping, on all fours. Roach recovered himself quickly and with a sharp downwards swing of the shield caught him on the back of his neck.

'The rabbit-blow!' said Augustus. 'I've never seen it done in an arena before, have you, my dear Livia? Eh? Killed him too, I swear.'

The Thessalian was dead. I expected Livia to be greatly displeased but all she said was: 'And served him right. That's what comes of underrating one's opponent. I'm disappointed in that net-man. Still, it has saved me that five hundred in gold, so I can't complain, I suppose.'

from *I Claudius* by Robert Graves

Questions

1　Which verbs describe the actions of the two men, when they first enter the arena? Explain the actions of the two men, and say what impression you get of each man because of them? Which verbs are used to describe the movements of the men at the beginning of the fight, which add to these impressions?

2　Claudius says, 'Soon the fight became more lively.' Make a list of the verbs which show the liveliness of the movements in the fight. In each case explain the appropriateness of the words chosen to describe the actions, and suggest any alternatives which you consider to be better.

3　Choose two sentences which, you feel, Robert Graves has constructed in order to suggest the nature of the movement involved. Quote the sentences and explain the effect of them.

Practice work Choose one of the following, and write the appropriate essay in which action of some sort must play a prominent part.

The Struggle
The Eleventh Hour
The Rough Crossing
The Last Train
The Bridge

Essay work Look at the following essay questions carefully. To describe any of these scenes or events you will need to **use the skills** you have learned in the descriptive section. Make sure that your description is detailed and made vivid by a suitable use of vocabulary and comparisons.

1 Write an essay with one of these titles:

The Parade
The Carnival
The Mill
The Attic
The Jumble Sale
The Races
The Disco

2 Over the doorway the date when it had been built had been carved in the elegant figures of the period, 1673, and the house, grey and weather beaten looked as much part of the landscape as the trees that sheltered it. I knocked again, and the door slowly opened.

Continue the essay by describing the interior of the house.

3 Choose one of the following quotations and write the essay suggested by it, developing the description of the scene and the season.

'The rain set early in to-night,
   The sullen wind was soon awake,
It tore the elm-tops down for spite,
   And did its worst to vex the lake:
I listened with heart fit to break.'

Robert Browning

'The full moon easterly rising, furious
Against a winter sky ragged with red;
The hedges high in snow, and owls raving – '

Robert Graves

'The day dispossessed of light. At four o'clock
in the afternoon, a sulphorous, manufactured
twilight, smudging the scummed lake's far side,
leant on the park. Sounds muffled –
as if the lolling much, clogged then at the source –
crawled to the ear.'

Tony Connor

'The silver birches are on fire
   With thin gold flame;
The sharp leaves of the briar
   Burn with a russet gleam;
The bramble rough with red
   Is a smouldering ember.'

John Smith

'Blown bubble-film blue, the sky wraps round
   Weeds of warm light whose every root and rod
Splutters with soapy green, and all the world
   Sweats with the bead of summer in its bud.'

Laurie Lee

3 Character writing

A good character description is one in which character is shown in a clear and interesting way. There are several ways of doing this and you should balance these techniques in your essays. Also use your characters to help form the plot of your narrative essays and plays. The events of the story will be determined by the particular characteristics of the people involved.

Describing character by: Statement

You can describe character in a straightforward way using statements. There are specific adjectives which describe character directly. Look at the following list, and check that you know the meaning of these words.

Vocabulary

domineering	introverted	irascible	benevolent
shrewd	extroverted	charismatic	malevolent
sensitive	superior	reticent	naïve
wily	arrogant	lethargic	morose
resourceful	withdrawn	garrulous	supercilious
boastful	resilient	melancholic	facetious
affected	taciturn	dogmatic	deferential
miserly	laconic	asinine	obsequious
candid	belligerent	mercenary	

Pictures   Look at the following pictures of people. Jot down the words from the list which could be used to describe each person's character. Add any appropriate adjectives which you can think of.

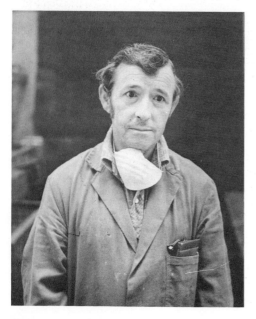 

Practice work   Write short, direct descriptions of each character.

Suggestion

By mentioning something specific about a person, you can suggest character. Read the following extracts.

1

Chamak was a gangling youth with a big nose crowned with a perpetual pimple which he wore like a trinket of jewellery. He polished his pimple and made it shine. He had curly hair which stuck out fiercely from the sides of his head and he always wore startling clothes: red and green bush shirts with luminous ties painted with Mickey Mouse and nude girls and palm trees.

The girl he was in love with was called Sushila. She was large and sturdy with a dark-green birth mark the size of a rupee on her cheek. Chamak said he thought she had lovely dimples, they bloomed when she smiled. Sushila never smiled. She was very stern and was known to us as 'Jhansi-ki-Rani', the revolutionary Joan of Arc who had fought and been defeated by the British in the Indian Mutiny.

from *Poona Company* by Farrukh Dhondy

2

Uncle Hammer was two years older than Papa and unmarried; he came every winter to spend the Christmas season with us. Like Papa, he had dark, red-brown skin, a square-jawed face, and high cheekbones; yet there was a great difference between them somehow. His eyes which showed a great warmth as he hugged and kissed us now, often had a cold, distant glaze, and there was an aloofness in him which the boys and I could never quite bridge.

from *Roll of Thunder, Hear My Cry* by Mildred D. Taylor

Questions

1 What does the writer suggest about Chamak's character when he says he had 'a perpetual pimple which he wore like a trinket of jewellery'?
2 What do Chamak's clothes show about his character?
3 What do the comments on Sushila's smiles show about her?
4 What are people suggesting about Sushila by calling her a 'revolutionary Joan of Arc'?
5 What is suggested about Uncle Hammer's character by the reference to his eyes?

The following longer extract shows how this technique can be extended to produce an effective and intriguing description.

The New Boy

Fanshaw was aware of the boy watching him and in the doorway he turned, looked back at the youngster. Their eyes met, their glances locked.

He was about fourteen years old, small in build but with a toughness and wiriness that suggested he could more than hold his own in older, bigger company. He was dressed in a ragged windcheater and faded jeans and his short cropped fair hair was untidy and spiky, as though he had slept out in the open. There was a certain deliberate ingenuousness*, an openness about his features that suggested to Fanshaw that the truth lay deep hidden behind; the boy would never display much emotion, his mouth would rarely smile, adults would despair of reaching him, touching anything behind that apparent innocence. He would keep his own counsel and control and show only what people wanted to see, while he retained his own independence and his own truths. But the blankness of his face was betrayed by the liveliness of his eyes. They were eyes that could hold and talk and

* ingenuousness – frankness, lack of deception

71

feel; their sharpness and intensity were remarkable; they would show a controlled passion, the coldness of anger, but never the markings of fear. Now they held a mild curiosity, overlaid with weary indifference.

from *A Violent Death* by Roy Lewis

Questions

1 What facts are we given about the boy?
2 What does the author suggest about the boy's character? Pick out some examples where the author states a fact about the boy and follows it up with what it suggests about his character.

Practice work

Complete the following statements in such a way as to suggest character.

Her dark eyes darted back and forth relentlessly suggesting . . .

His furrowed brow and hooded eyes conveyed . . .

She ordered the waiter in such a way as to suggest . . .

The way he slouched in his chair suggested . . .

The softness of her mouth and delicate, velvety eyes suggested . . .

Appearance

A person's character can be suggested by describing their physical appearance.

The Businessman

He was a substantial man of about forty eight to fifty, with shoulders, waist and hips all knocking forty four. The dinner jacket sat on him with the ease of a second skin, and when he shot his cuffs occasionally he did so without affectation, showing off noticeably well-manicured hands.

He had tidy grey-brown hair, straight eyebrows, narrow nose, small firm mouth, rounded freshly shaved chin, and very high unwrinkled lower eyelids, which gave him a secret, shuttered look.

from *Odds Against* by Dick Francis

The Fat Man

The man with the jay-bird voice strode back and forth in front of them. He was a big man with a short, thick neck. His cheeks puffed and jiggled as he walked. Julilly noticed that his fingers puffed, too, over the whip that he flicked in his hand. He had a toothpick in his mouth that stuck between two yellow teeth. Julilly didn't like his oily skin. His faded brown hair was tangled and dirty, his baggy pants were streaked with drippings and his little eyes were green and sly.

from *Underground to Canada* by Barbara Smucker

Questions

What do the writers suggest about the characters by the following references to appearance?

'with shoulders, waist and hips all knocking forty four'

'with the ease of a second skin'

'well-manicured hands'

'which gave him a secret, shuttered look'

'cheeks puffed and jiggled as he walked'

'two yellow teeth'

'his faded brown hair was tangled and dirty'

'his little eyes were green and sly'

Picture Look at the picture. Choose two of the people and describe their appearance in such a way as to suggest their characters.

Action

Another way of conveying character is by describing actions. You need to give a detailed description of the way a character does something or the particular habits he or she has.

In the following extract, the author takes the simple activity of getting up in the morning but describes it in such a way as to show a great deal about character.

Mr Mitterman

As he did every other morning of the year, James Mitterman, chartered accountant, folded back the sheet and the blanket covering him to a precise forty-five degrees. Only the slight indentation on the pillow betrayed the fact that he had slept there for the past eight hours.

Slipping on his paisley-patterned dressing gown, he listened a moment at his wife's door before making his way to the bathroom to perform his ritual ablutions. The warm sun flooding through the opaque window, caused him to pause and open the casement. Just in time to catch the newspaper boy (James could never remember their names) riding up the circular tarmac drive. The lad caught the movement at the window.

'Sorry, Mr Mitterman – no *Financial Times* again today. Brought you the *The Times* instead.'

'Thank you.' Mitterman inclined his head gravely. Sometimes he considered the inconvenience of living in the country hardly worth its benefits. Slowly he divested himself of his pyjamas, noting with approval the matching green against the dressing gown. Really, Marks and Spencers did a fine job these days. Mitterman, for all his immaculate habits, was never ashamed of saving money. He bent to his daily exercises.

from *The Village Cricket Match* by John Parker

Questions

1 What kind of person would 'fold back the sheets to a precise forty-five degrees' and leave 'only the slight indentation on the pillow'?

2 What does 'Slowly he divested himself of his pyjamas' show about his character?

3 What impression of Mr Mitterman is conveyed by phrases such as 'ritual ablutions' and 'daily exercises'?

4 What kind of person would 'note with approval the matching green against the dressing gown'?

Practice work

Write a paragraph describing each of the following actions being done by a different type of person. Choose your words carefully in order to describe their characters through their actions.

eating

arriving home from school or work

shopping

Comparisons

My Uncle and Aunt

I was staying at the time with my uncle and his wife. Although she was my aunt, I never thought of her as anything but the wife of my uncle, partly because he was so big and trumpeting and red-hairy and used to fill every inch of the hot little house like an old buffalo squeezed into an airing cupboard, and partly because she was so small and silk and quick and made no noise at all as she whisked about on padded paws, dusting the china dogs, feeding the buffalo, setting the mousetraps that never caught her; and once she cleared out of the room, to squeak in a nook or nibble in the hayloft, you forgot she had ever been there.

But there he was, always a steaming hulk of an uncle, his braces straining like hausers, crammed behind the counter of the tiny shop at the front of the house, and breathing like a brass band; or guzzling and blustery in the kitchen over his gutsy supper, too big for everything except the great black boats of his boots. As he ate, the house grew smaller; he billowed out over the furniture, the loud check meadow of his waistcoat littered, as though after a picnic, with cigarette ends, peelings, cabbage stalks, birds' bones, gravy; and the forest fire of his hair crackled among the hooked hams from the ceiling. She was so small she could hit him only if she stood on a chair, and every Saturday night at half past ten he would lift her up under his arm on to a chair in the kitchen so that she could hit him on the head with whatever was handy, which was always a china dog.

from *A Prospect of the Sea* by Dylan Thomas

77

Explain each of the following comparisons and say what it suggests about the character.

He '**used to fill every inch of the hot little house like an old buffalo squeezed into an airing cupboard**'.

'**a steaming hulk of an uncle**'

'**breathing like a brass band**'

'**the forest fire of his hair crackled among the hooked hams**'

'**she was so small and silk and quick and made no noise at all as she whisked about on padded paws**'

'**to squeak in a nook or nibble in the hayloft, you forgot she had ever been there**'

Soli

One regular customer was Soli Kolmi, a baron of the Chowk. It wasn't his real name at all, but Kolmi, a 'prawn', was what he was known as, because he was constantly bent double with a crooked back. He had a long nose and a vulturous neck, supple enough to allow him to hold his head up, and he wore a black felt cap on his thinning hair. He was scrawny and had deep-hooded eyes like a bird.

from *Poona Company* by Farrukh Dhondy

Questions

1 Why is Soli Kolmi nicknamed 'prawn'?
2 What comparison does the writer use to describe Soli Kolmi?
3 Which words and phrases develop the comparison?

Practice work Develop the following sentences into paragraphs in which the original simile or metaphor is extended.
He approached his opponent **like a lion stalking its prey** . . .
His skin was wrinkled **like the bark of an old tree** . . .
The dancer swayed gently **like a flower in a breeze** . . .
The clearing of his throat sounded **like a stubborn car engine loath to start** . . .

Speech

Dialogue must be used effectively to show character but it requires careful handling. It should only be used when either the content or the tone shows something about the character who is speaking.

Study the following extracts of speech. What kind of character is involved in each?

'Hi, there! I'm Alex Smith, but that's a bit heavy, so how about you just call me Al. I'll be around this place for a while so let's lay a few things on the line. I want you to know that while I'm teaching you biology and eco-sciences, anything you want to say is fine by me. I've been through the school scene, and I can handle it . . . .'

'Oh well done Caroline! . . . That's the spirit! . . . Oh well dribbled ! Now tackle, Caroline, tackle! . . . Well if she won't get out of your way use your hockey stick! . . . Oh really Caroline — it's only a drop of blood . . . don't make such a fuss, we'll look at you at half-time . . . Come on St Matilda's . . .'

'Right you ugly lot! . . . page 87 – Tudors and Stuarts. You! – Baxter – name me a Stuart! Rod Stewart, eh? You think that's clever, do you? You think I stay up all night preparing work for half-witted morons like you to come in and make stupid jokes? Well you'd better understand this, Baxter, you're wrong, so very wrong . . .'

'Well, I thought we'd try Venn diagrams today, er, if that's agreeable, what do you say? No? You don't want to have a go at New Maths, Sebastian? I'm sorry, I mean Spike . . . Well, that's fair enough . . . . No, no, I'm sure we'll find some other time, when we're all in the right frame of mind . . . What do you think'

When using direct speech the verb or adverb used to indicate how something was said plays an important part in showing character. What difference in character is suggested by changing the verb of saying in the following sentences?

'Is it time to go?' she demanded.

'Is it time to go?' she moaned

'Is it time to go'? she shrieked.

Practice work

1 Make a list of as many verbs and adverbs of saying as you can. Arrange them into groups which convey similar characters.

2 Supply the direct speech to complete the following.

'. . . . . .' she wheedled.

'. . . . . .' she debated.

'. . . . . .' she expressed contemptuously.

'. . . . . .' he muttered sulkily.

'. . . . . .' she exclaimed irately.

'. . . . . .' he rebuked sharply.

3 Fill in verbs and adverbs of saying to complete the following passage from Dylan Thomas's *Holiday Memory*.

'Uncle Owen says he can't find the bottle opener,' . . .

'Has he looked under the hallstand?' . . .

'Willy's cut his finger,' . . .

'Got your spade?' . . .

'If somebody doesn't kill that dog,' . . .

'Uncle Owen says why should the bottle opener be under the hallstand?' . . .

'Never again, never again,' . . .

'I know I put the pepper somewhere,' . . .

'Willy's bleeding,' . . .

'Look, there's a bootlace in my bucket,' . . .

'Oh come on, come on,' . . .

'Let's have a look at the bootlace in your bucket,' . . .

'If I lay my hands on that dog,' . . .

'Uncle Owen's found the bottle opener,' . . .

'Willy's bleeding over the cheese,' . . .

Read the following carefully. Write a character study of Mr Proudham and Mr Sleight, showing how their characters are conveyed.

My Neighbours

But when I opened the front gate of the house Mr Proudham and Mr Sleight were looking. It was almost dark and they had not put the light on in their ground floor window. They stood side by side, shadowy, improbable figures. I was to see them like that so often during the weeks to come – Mr Proudham, immensely tall and etiolated, with a thin head and unhealthy, yellowish skin: and Mr Sleight, perhaps five feet one or two, with a benevolent rather stupid moon of a face. He was bald: Mr Proudham had dingy-white hair, worn rather long.

They went out three times a day, at ten, at two and at six. In addition, Mr Proudham went out at eleven each morning carrying a shopping bag of drab olive cloth. And it was in a shop, Cox's Mini-Market that I first came face to face with him. He was buying parsnips and because I was standing at the back of the queue I had a chance to study him. He was considerably older than I had at first thought, with heavy-lidded eyes that drooped at the corners and a mouth very full of teeth. On top of the off-white hair he wore a curious woollen beret, rather like that of a French onion-seller but with a pompom on the top. As he turned to leave the shop he saw me. He stopped. Then, as though he had considered the situation carefully, he bowed, and lifted his hand. For a moment I wondered if he were going to raise the little woollen hat. But he only gave a half-salute.

from *Mr Proudham and Mr Sleight* by Susan Hill

Using character in stories and plays

> The events of a story and its outcome may be determined by a person's character as the following story and play show.

The Fury

There were times when Mrs Fletcher was sure her husband thought more of his rabbits than anything else in the world: more than tobacco and comfort, more than her – or the other woman. And this was one of those times, this Saturday morning as she looked out from the kitchen where she was preparing the dinner to where she could see Fletcher working absorbedly, and grooming his two favourite Angoras for the afternoon's show in Cressley.

She was a **passionate** woman who **clung single-mindedly to what was hers** and was **prepared to defend her rights with vigour**. While courting Fletcher she had drawn blood on an erstwhile rival who had threatened to reassert her claims. Since then she had had worse things to contend with. Always, it seemed to her, there was something between her and her rightful possession of Fletcher. At the moment it was the rabbits. The big shed had been full of hutches at one time, but now Fletcher concentrated his attention on a handful of animals in which he had a steady faith. But there were still too many for Mrs Fletcher, who **resented sharing him with anything or anybody**, and the sight of his absorption now stirred feelings which brought unnecessary force to bear **on the sharp knife** with which she sliced potatoes for the pan.

'Got a special class for Angoras today,' Fletcher said later at the table.

Mrs Fletcher gave no sign of interest. She said, 'D'you think you'll be back in time for t'pictures?'

Fletcher gulped water. He had a way of drinking which showed his fine teeth. 'Should be,' he answered between swallows. 'Anyway, if you're so keen to go why don't you fix up with Mrs Sykes?'

'I should be able to go out with you, Saturday nights,' Mrs Fletcher said.

'Anyway I'll try me best. Can't say fairer than that, can I?' Fletcher said dryly.

'Not as long as you get back in time.'

Fletcher pushed back his chair and stood up. 'I don't see why not. It shouldn't be a long job today. It isn't a big show. I should be back by half past seven at latest.'

'Well, just see 'at you are,' she said.

She stood by the window and watched him go down the road in the pale sunshine, carrying case, slung from one shoulder, prevented from jogging by a careful hand. He cut a handsome, well-set-up figure when he was dressed up, she thought. **Often too handsome, too well-set-up for her peace of mind.**

By half past seven she was washed, dressed and lightly made-up ready for the evening out. But Fletcher had not returned. And when the clock on the mantelshelf chimed eight there was still no sign of him. It was after ten when he came. She was sitting by the fire, the wireless blaring unheard, her knitting needles flashing with silent fury.

'What time d'you call this?' she said, giving him no chance to speak. 'Saturday night an' me sittin' here like a doo-lal while you gallivant up an' down as you please.'

He was obviously uneasy, expecting trouble. 'I'm sorry,' he said. 'I meant to be back. I thought I should but there were more than I expected. It took a long time...' He avoided her eyes as he went into the passage to hang up his overcoat. 'Didn't win owt either,' he muttered half to himself. 'Not a blink' sausage.'

'You knew I specially wanted to see that picture, didn't you?' Mrs Fletcher said, her voice rising. 'I've been telling you all week, but that makes no difference, does it! **What does your wife matter once you get off with your blasted rabbits, eh?'**

As though he had not heard her Fletcher opened the case and lifted out one of the rabbits and held it to him, stroking the long soft fur. 'You just wasn't good enough, was you, eh?' The rabbit blinked its pink eyes in the bright electric light. 'Nivver mind: you're a beauty all t'same.'

His ignoring of her maddened Mrs Fletcher almost more than she could bear. 'I'm talking to you!' she stormed.

'I heard you; an' I said I'm sorry. What more do you want?'

'Oh, you're sorry, and that's the end of it, I suppose. That's all my Saturday night's worth, is it?'

'I couldn't help it,' Fletcher said. 'I said I couldn't help it.' He put the rabbit back in the case and sat down to unlace his shoes. She watched him, eyes glittering, mouth a thin trap of temper.

'Aye, you said so. You said you'd be home at half past seven an' all, and we've seen what that was worth. How do I know what you've been up to while I've been sitting here by myself?'

He looked quickly up at her, his usual full colour deepening and spreading. 'What're you gettin' at now?'

'You know what I'm gettin' at.' Her head nodded grimly.

Fletcher threw down his shoes. 'I told you,' he said with throaty anger, 'an' that's all over. It's been finished with a long time. Why can't you let it rest, 'stead o' keeping harping on about it?'

He stood up, and taking the carrying case, walked out in his slippers to the shed, leaving her to talk to the empty room. He always got away from her like that. **She grabbed the poker and stabbed savagely at the fire.**

On Sunday morning she was shaking a mat in the yard when her neighbour spoke to her over the fence.

'Did you get to the Palace this week, then, Mrs Fletcher?' Mrs Sykes asked her. 'Oh, but you did miss a treat. All about the early Christians and the cloak 'at Jesus wore on the cross. Lovely, it was, and ever so sad.'

'I wanted to see it,' Mrs Fletcher said, 'but Jim didn't get back from Cressley till late. His rabbits y'know.' **She felt a strong desire to abuse him in her talk, but pride held her tongue.** It was bad enough his being as he was **without the shame of everyone's knowing it.**

'Oh, aye, they had a show, didn't they?' Mrs Sykes said. 'Aye, I saw him in the bus station afterwards. He was talking to a woman I took to be your sister.'

Mrs Fletcher shot the other woman a look. What was she up to? She knew very well that her sister had lived down south these last twelve months. Her cheeks flamed suddenly and she turned her back on her neighbour and went into the house.

Fletcher was lounging, unshaven and in shirt sleeves, his feet propped up on the fireplace, reading the Sunday papers. She went for him as soon as she had put the thickness of the door between them and Mrs Sykes, who still lingered in the yard.

'You must think I'm stupid!'

'Eh?' Fletcher said, looking up. 'What's up now?'

'What's up? What's up? How can you find the face to sit there with your feet up and ask me that? You must think I'm daft altogether; but it's you 'at's daft, if you did but know it. Did you think you could get away with it? Did you really think so? You might ha' known somebody 'ud see you. And you had to do it in the bus station at that – a public place!'

'I don't even know what you're talking about,' Fletcher said, but his eyes gave him away.

'You'll brazen it out to the very end, won't you?' she said. 'You liar you. "Oh, I've made a mistake," he says. "I'll never see her again," he says. And what do you do but go running back to her the minute you think you can get away with it!'

Fletcher got up, throwing the newspaper to one side. 'I tell you I don't – ' Then he stopped, the bluster draining out of him. 'All right,' he said quietly. 'If you'll calm down a minute I'll tell you.'

'You'll tell *me*!' Mrs Fletcher said. 'You'll tell me nothing any more. It's all lies, lies, lies every time you open your mouth. Well I've finished. Bad enough your rabbits, but I draw the line at fancy women. You promised me faithful you wouldn't see her again. You said it sitting in that very chair. And what was it worth, eh? Not a row o' buttons. **What d'you think I feel like when me own neighbours tell me** they've seen you carryin' on?'

'If you wouldn't listen so much to what t'neighbours say an' take notice o' what I have to tell you – ' Fletcher began.

'I've done listening to you,' she said. 'Now I'm having my say.'

'Well, you'll say it to yourself, and rest o' t'street mebbe, but not to me.' He strode across the room and dragged down his coat. 'I'll go somewhere where I can talk to somebody 'at's not next door to a ravin' lunatic.'

'And stop there when you got there,' she told him. 'Go to her. Tell her I've had enough of you. See if she'll sit at home while you traipse about countryside with a boxful o' mucky vermin.'

He was at the door, pulling on his coat.

'And take your things,' she said. 'Might as well make a clean sweep while you're about it.'

'I'm going to our Tom's,' he said. 'I'll send for 'em tomorrow.'

'I'll have 'em ready,' she said.

When the door had closed behind him she stood for a moment, eyes glittering, nostrils dilated, her entire body stiff and quivering with rage. **Then suddenly she plucked a vase from the mantelshelf and dashed it to pieces in the hearth. She clenched and unclenched her hands at her sides, her eyes seeking wildly as the fury roared impotently in her.**

At half past ten she was in the kitchen making her supper when she heard the front door open. She went through into the passage and her hand tightened involuntarily about the milk bottle she was holding as she saw Fletcher there.

'Well,' she said. 'Have you come for your things?' Her voice was tight and unnatural and Fletcher took it as a sign of her lingering anger.

He closed the door and stood sheepishly behind it, his eyes avoiding hers. 'I just thought I'd come an' see if you'd calmed down,' he said. 'It'd ha' been all right if only you'd listened to me.'

'I never expected you to come back,' she said, and moved almost trance-like, across the room to the fire, **still watching him intently almost disbelievingly**, as though she had expected that with his slamming of the door this morning he would walk off the edge of the world, never to be seen again.

He came over to the hearth to stand beside her. He started to put his hand on her shoulder, but as she moved away slightly he dropped his arm again and looked past her into the fire.

'What I said before, I meant,' he said, speaking quietly, earnestly, with the awkwardness of a man not used to expressing the finer feelings. 'I could ha' told you last night, only I didn't see any point. It was all forgotten as far as I was concerned. Finished. But she was waiting for me when I came out o' show. I told her I didn't want to see her again. There was never owt much between us anyway. But I couldn't get rid of her. She hung on like mad. An' when I looked at her, all painted an' powdered up, I found meself thinkin' what a great fool I'd been ever to risk losing all that mattered for a brazen baggage like her. It took me a couple of hours to get rid of her. She got proper nasty towards the end. Started shoutin' and swearin', right in the street. It was awful.' Fletcher sighed and shook his head and a shudder seemed to run through Mrs Fletcher. 'And I had to jump on a bus in the end and just leave her standing there. There was nowt else I could do bar give her a clout or summat . . .'

As he finished talking something **seemed to snap inside Mrs Fletcher and she began to cry softly**. He put his arm round her shoulders, tentatively at first, then, when she offered no resistance with pressure, drawing her to him.

'Now, lass. Now, then. Cryin' won't do any good. We've had our little bust-up, an' now it's all over an' done with.'

'Oh, why didn't I listen?' she sobbed. 'None of this would have happened then.'

He drew her down into an armchair and held her to him. 'Never mind now, lass. No harm done. Don't cry any more.'

After a time, he said, 'I'll just nip out an' see to the rabbits, then we can get off to bed.'

She held him to her. 'No leave 'em. Come to bed now.'

He smiled quietly, indulgently. 'Still a bit jealous, eh? Well I reckon they'll manage till morning.'

Later still, in the dark secret warmth of the bed, she clung to him again. 'Did you mean it?' she said. 'When you said you loved nobody but me?'

'I did,' he said.

'Say it, then,' she said, holding him hard.

'I love you, lass,' he said. 'Nobody but you. It'll be better in future. You'll see.'

She could have cried out then. Better in future! Oh, why hadn't she listened? Why, why, why? If only she had listened and heard him in time! For this moment was all she had. There could be no future: nothing past the morning when he would go out and find the rabbits slaughtered in their hutches.

Stan Barstow

Questions

1 What kind of character is Mrs Fletcher? Give evidence from the story. Some parts are in **bold** type to help you.
2 What signs are there of her violent tendencies before we find out about the rabbits?
3 Explain how the plot is determined by Mrs Fletcher's character.

Practice work   Choose one of the following. Make a plan and rough draft developing character, setting and plot. Write a story in which the plot is clearly determined by the character.

1

Martin drew the cloth from the kitchen table, folded it and laid it on a chair. After the anxious fuss of putting his brother and sister to bed he lifted his books from the cupboard and spread them over the bare wood, where they would stay till the heart-catching click of the gate-latch signalled his parents' return. Most of the books had been stolen.

from *A Time to Keep* by Alan Sillitoe

2

Alison Temple stood at her kitchen sink washing up. It was always the first chore of her day, and with the ease of long practice she flicked her cloth around the cups and across the saucers and plates. It was not a job that required much concentration and only half her mind was on what she was doing, for the 8.03 from Sutton Street was due at any moment and she was listening for the first sounds of its approach.

from *The Woman in the Green Dress* by Joyce Marsh

Plays

In play writing, your major means of showing characters is through what they say and how they say it. The script must be set out in a special way. The following extract shows you how to do this.

The Reunion

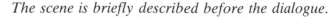

The scene is briefly described before the dialogue.

In the background sounds of a small café – a gentle tinkle of cups, and a discreet murmur of hushed voices. The door opens, and there is a sudden burst of traffic noise from the street outside. The door is slammed shut.

LIZ *breathes heavily – the wheezing pant of a fat woman, who has been hurrying. The panting becomes a sigh of relief as she sinks into a chair.*

The names of characters speaking appear on the left hand side of the page.	

WAITRESS I'm afraid you can't sit at the table by the window, madam.

LIZ I'll have a cup of coffee.

WAITRESS If you wouldn't mind moving.

A new line is used to indicate each new speaker.

LIZ Strong, black and without froth.

WAITRESS I'll be glad to serve you at another table.

LIZ (*mockingly*) You wouldn't be glad to serve me anywhere. I saw your face when I waltzed in. Dropped like an old sack. Make your customers proper welcome, don't you?

WAITRESS We cater for a high class trade. Select people come for coffee in this café.

Advice to actors on how to speak or present the character is given in brackets before the words to be spoken.

LIZ (*getting angry*) I know what's wrong wi' you. You don't want anybody to peep through the window, and see me picking my nose. Might put 'em off. Know how long it is since I had a wash? Nor do I. I bet I stink. Where's that coffee?

WAITRESS This table . . .

LIZ Know where I've just come from? Court. Do you know what the beak did? Fined me for being drunk and disorderly . . . 'You again?' His first words 'You again,' he says. 'Floggin's too good for you, you drunken old baggage.' P'raps they weren't his exact words, but that's what he meant. So he fines me . . . Know what for? Aiming a pint pot at his barman. Missed him, though. Pity. But do you know why I threw that for? . . . He wouldn't serve me . . . Cup of coffee. Please. (*The door opens and shuts.*)

Stage directions and sound effects are given in brackets in the centre of the page, between speeches.

Read the rest of the extract and answer the questions which follow.

WAITRESS	Good morning, sir.
EDDIE	Oh. Good – good morning.
WAITRESS	Table for one, sir? over in the corner.
EDDIE	I – er – I'll . . . I'll sit here, if you don't mind. By the window.
WAITRESS	That seat is . . .
EDDIE	Could I? Would you bring me a cup of coffee? Please.
WAITRESS	(*sotto voice*) Some people!
EDDIE	Liz . . .
LIZ	You can't sit here. This table is reserved.
EDDIE	You didn't have to, you know. I mean – run away from me as if – as if . . .
LIZ	I'm not in the habit of talking to strange men.
EDDIE	I – I thought I'd lost you. Then I saw you through this window.
LIZ	If a lady can't have a coffee without being accosted, I don't know what the place is coming to.
EDDIE	I was there. I heard . . . They didn't give you half a chance. The magistrate didn't even listen.
LIZ	I can feel a draught. Somebody's mouth must be hanging open.
EDDIE	I shut up shop this morning. I went straight round to the Court as soon as I heard. I thought you might – sort of – need me. The fine, for instance. If you hadn't got enough for the fine, they might've locked you up.
LIZ	In a hole dead as this, there ought to be some peace and quiet.
EDDIE	I missed you on the way out. Different entrances.
LIZ	Is there a copper about? I've got a chap here making suggestions.
EDDIE	I only wanted to make sure that – that you were all right.
LIZ	Have you done forcing your attentions on me?
EDDIE	I'll go. If you really want me to.
LIZ	Oh, sit where you are, you wet lump of tripe.
EDDIE	You admit that we know each other then?
LIZ	Well, if it isn't Eddie. Old Eddie George . . . I'd sooner see the devil any day than your gormless mug.

(*There is a rattle of cups, ending with a thud as a tray is put on the table.*)

WAITRESS	Two coffees.
EDDIE	Oh – thanks.
WAITRESS	Enjoying the view?
LIZ	Sarky cat.
WAITRESS	Really!
LIZ	Pass the sugar . . . Well, were you satisfied?
EDDIE	What with?
LIZ	The show. I saw you. In the public gallery, along with all the other old perishers. It's warm, dry and free. It was the first time for you, wasn't it? You missed all my other performances. The reporters like me, anyway. I liven their day up. 'Call Elizabeth Warton.' Laughter in Court. The beak said I could be done for contempt. Contempt! I'd have spit in his eye, only me mouth was like a sandpit. (*She takes a noisy sip of coffee.*) I hope you enjoyed yourself.
EDDIE	It was – hell. Stuck up there. Not being able to do anything – to help
LIZ	Help?
EDDIE	That's why I followed you. I want . . . You can't go on like this.
LIZ	Who says?
EDDIE	I want to do something for you. I mean – if only for old time's sake. It's daft – us both living in the same town and never . . . It's not as if we'd ever quarrelled, or . . . I want to help.
LIZ	The only way anybody can help me is out of this world. I'm sick of it. I've tried long enough to fix myself with booze, only that's not strong enough. Do you think this coffee might do the trick? Smells as though the stuck-up cat mixed it with disinfectant. I'm worn out. Time I was traded in for a new model . . . Don't stare like that or your eyes'll drop out. What's the matter wi' me? Tide mark showing?
EDDIE	You haven't changed, Liz. Not really. You haven't changed a bit. You're still the girl I – I . . .
LIZ	No, I'm not. So you can stop your goggling. Give me the flaming willies. Reminding me where I've gone wrong.
EDDIE	Your hair . . .
LIZ	Hasn't been washed for years. And my beautiful blue eyes are bloodshot. I'm an old bag, and you needn't rub it in.

EDDIE	You're Liz.
LIZ	The girl you knew's been smothered under fifteen stone of fat. If you don't recognise that you're softer than I took you for. Drink your coffee, and get out.
EDDIE	Do you know what this place is? Do you?
LIZ	Don't try to make me sorry for myself. I deserved all I got.
EDDIE	This is the place where I – first met you.
LIZ	Don't be gormless. It hasn't been built more than a couple of years.
EDDIE	It was – open ground then. The town had hardly pushed out this far. You must remember.
LIZ	Are you trying to make my flesh creep?
EDDIE	There was a – bit of a brook. It ran just about where those tables are now. They must have – what d'you call it? – pushed it out of the way – diverted it. And there were trees.
LIZ	Shut up, will you? You're worse than a hangover. Shut up.
EDDIE	It was a Sunday afternoon.
LIZ	What was?
EDDIE	When I met you.
LIZ	I knew you'd be off like this. I kept out of your way while I could.
EDDIE	Not long after the Great War it would be. Not more than a few years anyway. About 1920.
LIZ	Slobber, slobber, slobber.
EDDIE	You wouldn't have been more than sixteen. With funny long skirts, and your hair flying wild.
LIZ	If you don't give over, I'll let you have this coffee. Straight between the eyes.
EDDIE	I was only trying to – remind you.
LIZ	You're making me sick. Counting cherry stones. Picking daisy petals. You needn't trouble yourself: I can give you the answer now. It's 'she loves me not'.
EDDIE	Forty years ago. Here. Right here.
LIZ	It don't do any good to remember.

from *Don't Wait For Me* by David Campton

1 What do we find out about the characters of Liz, Eddie and the Waitress from:

what each person says?

what the other characters say about them?

how they move or behave?

the advice given to the actors in the script?

2 Give a brief account of the plot so far. Using the clues provided by Liz and Eddie about their background and what you have found out about their characters, outline the possible development of the rest of the plot.

Practice work

Look at the following opening to a play. Make notes on what you find out about the setting, characters and plot. Then continue the script in a manner which develops both character and plot to some satisfactory conclusion. Remember to use the different types of endings you learned in the narrative section.

Time To Put Your Foot Down!

The living room of the Pearson family. Afternoon. It is a comfortably furnished, much lived-in room in a small suburban semi-detached villa. Mrs Pearson and Mrs Fitzgerald are sitting opposite each other at a small table, on which are two teacups and saucers and the cards with which Mrs Fitzgerald has been telling Mrs Pearson's fortune.

MRS FITZGERALD   (*collecting up the cards*) And that's all I can tell you, Mrs Pearson. Could be a good fortune. Could be a bad one. All depends on yourself now. Make up your mind – and there it is.

MRS PEARSON   Yes, thank you, Mrs Fitzgerald. I'm much obliged, I'm sure. It's wonderful having a real fortune teller living next door. Did you learn that out East, too?

MRS FITZGERALD   I did. Twelve years I had of it, with my old man rising to be Lieutenant Quartermaster. He learnt a lot, and I learnt a lot more. But will you make up your mind now, Mrs Pearson dear? Put your foot down, once an' for all, an' be the mistress of your own house an' the boss of your own family.

MRS PEARSON   (*smiling apologetically*) That's easier said than done. Besides I'm so fond of them even if they are so thoughtless and selfish. They don't mean to be ...

MRS FITZGERALD   No doubt about it at all. Who's the better for being spoilt – grown man, lad or girl? Nobody. You think it does 'em good when you run after them all the time, take their orders as if you were the servant in the house, stay at home every night while they go out enjoying themselves? Never in all your life. It's the ruin of them as well as you. Husbands, sons, daughters should be taking notice of wives an' mothers, not giving 'em orders an' treating 'em like dirt. An' don't tell me you don't know what I mean, for I know more than you've told me.

MRS PEARSON   (*dubiously*) I – keep dropping a hint ...

MRS FITZGERALD   Hint? It's more than hints your family needs, Mrs Pearson.

MRS PEARSON   (*dubiously*) I suppose it is. But I do hate any unpleasantness. And it's so hard to know where to start. I keep making up my mind to have it out with them – but somehow I don't know how to begin. (*She glances at her watch or at a clock.*) Oh – good gracious! Look at the time. Nothing ready and they'll be home any minute – and probably all in a hurry to go out again.

As she is about to rise, MRS FITZGERALD *reaches out across the table and pulls her down.*

MRS FITZGERALD   Let 'em wait or look after themselves for once. This is where your foot goes down. Start now. (*She lights a cigarette from the one she has just finished.*)

from *Mother's Day* by J B Priestley

Practice work

Picture

Look carefully at the following picture. It is the setting for a play. Jot down notes to the following questions before you begin.

Who are the two people in the scene?

What kind of characters have they?

What action is going to take place?

What will the plot be?

What will be the point or purpose of the play?

Essay work   Look at the following essay questions carefully. To write any of these you need to **use the skills** you have learned in this chapter. This means using appropriate adjectives and comparisons. You will also need to suggest character by referring to actions, habits and speech. Sometimes you will need to use the characters to develop the plot of a story or a play.

1

Three men were ordered into a line behind the cart. They stood like broken trees, their hands dangling like willow branches in the wind. Julilly knew each one.

There was Ben, solid and strong and as black as midnight. He could chop a woodpile higher than his head when the others still had little mounds up to their knees.

There was kind, gentle Adam whose singing was low as the sightless hollow of a tree. And there was Lester, the mulatto with speckly skin and angry eyes.

from *Underground to Canada* by Barbara Smucker

Write a story in which the plot revolves round these three characters.

2

She was a very tall, thin, beaky woman, and her eyes looked as though they'd been put in with two sooty fingers, all black all round. She'd always looked very sad – there was a great sadness about her.

from *The Cream of the Country* by Ken Whitmore

Write a story in which this woman is the main character.

3

My Uncle Ben used to drink in The Eagle. As if in memory, I would sometimes see him on summer Sunday afternoons, conducting the playing of 'pitch and toss' outside, or laughing at the Salvation Army Band whining on the disused tram tracks. He owned two of the new betting shops in Kirby and a sweets and tobacconist's on the block opposite The Eagle.

from *Ba, Ba, Black Sheep*, by Alan Bleasdale

Describe a man or a woman in your neighbourhood who is well-known because of his or her behaviour.

Describe a visit to the doctor or dentist in such a way as to bring out the person's character.

4

'Someone I never hope to meet again.' Describe such a person. You will need to describe the person's appearance, actions and speech to account for your reaction.

5

'A man doesn't know what he'll do, a man doesn't know what he is until he's put under extreme pressure.'

Write a play describing a person in such a situation, showing his character through his behaviour.

6

'Two men were looking through the bars,
One saw the mud, the other saw the stars.'

Write a play involving these two characters, showing their different views on life.

4 Personal writing

Personal writing involves writing about your own experience, or expressing your own opinions. Your style of writing should be lively and you should provide a suitable structure in which to write about your memories. When you are writing about your opinions you need to arrange your ideas carefully, and express them clearly.

Giving a factual account

The simplest way to write about your memories is to give the facts as you remember them.

My Life in Brighton

I was born fifty-eight years ago in Hove, the second child of a family of seven. My earliest recollection is that other children seemed to be better off than we were. But our parents cared so much for us. One particular thing that I always remember was that every Sunday morning my father used to bring us a comic and a bag of sweets. You used to be able to get a comic for a halfpenny plain, and a penny coloured. Sometimes now when I look back at it, I wonder how he managed to do it when he was out of work, and there was no money at all coming in.

My father was a painter and decorator. Sort of general odd-job man. He could do almost anything: repair roofs or do a bit of plastering; but painting and paper hanging were his main work. Yet in the neighbourhood where we lived there was hardly any work in the winter. People didn't want their houses done up then: they couldn't be painted outside and they didn't want the bother of having it all done up inside. So the winters were the hardest time.

from *Below Stairs* by Margaret Powell

Questions

1 What kind of information does the writer give us?
2 What kind of details does she leave out?
3 How could she have made the events of Sunday morning seem more interesting and important?

Practice work

Jot down some of the facts which you remember from your childhood. Organise them into a paragraph giving a factual account of your early memories.

Suggesting atmosphere

When asked to describe an event or a place you remember well suggest the atmosphere associated with it. The following extracts show how this is done.

The Pit

The pit-heads were bleak and lonely, yet awesome and exciting at the same time, like a lot of inside-feelings mixed up inside your mind together. The largest pit was building a mountain of tack-bank cinders and earth and bat-coal all jumbled in together and laid seam upon seam. You got the feeling that the mountain of slag and rubbish was alive and moving, moving at a sly rate that didn't show when you looked at it. But when you looked away and then looked back at it, you knew that it had moved forwards a bit. Moved and spread. That's how it looked, and you felt in time the whole mountain would have moved and spread forwards enough to swamp the valley it poised over. On top of the mountain was a narrow-gauge railtrack, and waggons of rubbish came away from the pit-workings along these tracks, to be tipped over the edge. The track-waggons, the pit-dobbins, were toylike all that way up. They looked like matchboxes, and the men working with them were little dolls dotting the slag-scape. The pit-wheel in its scaffold of derrick was a big one, towering over its cagehole black and creaking. The rope-wires running back to the cagehouse hummed with wind and strain. A lot of men worked in this pit. It was one of the few that stayed in full production, and the men worked hard in it so's not to be laid off in favour of somebody else. I tried to imagine them there under the earth cutting and hauling off, and the pit ponies pulling the lines up coal-filled carts towards the cage so's it could be winched up. Some pit ponies were topside in the colliery fields and getting themselves fettled up on grass and fresh air. They peered at us as if they were nearly blind ... and Gyp said they were.

from *Summer's End* by Archie Hill

Father's Study

I retain one confused impression from my earliest years; it is all red and black and warm. Our apartment was red: the upholstery was of red moquette, the Renaissance dining room was red, the figured silk hangings over the stained-glass doors were red, and the velvet curtains in Papa's study were red too. The furniture in this awful sanctum was made of black pear wood; I used to creep into the kneehole under the desk and envelop myself in its dusty glooms; it was dark and warm and the red of the carpet rejoiced my eyes. That is how I seem to have passed the early days of infancy. Safely ensconced, I watched, I touched, I took stock of the world.

from *Memoirs of a Dutiful Daughter* by Simone de Beauvoir

Questions

1 Why were these places important to the writers?
2 Carefully describe the atmosphere of each place. Refer to specific words or phrases, used in each, to suggest the atmosphere.

Practice work

Describe a place which was important to you as a child in such a way that the atmosphere of the place is clearly brought out.

Conveying emotion

When you are describing an event or an incident from your childhood you can make it more interesting if you try to describe the emotion caused by it. Read the following two extracts.

School Days

The Kirkwall Burgh School was a big school with a large staff and several hundred scholars. I did not hate it as I had hated the school in Wyre: I no longer tried to push on the hands of the clock with my will; the feeling of imprisonment faded, since part of my mind now agreed with school: I had begun to grow up. Yet there were months on end when I dreaded, morning after morning, as separate things for each seemed fatal, the setting out from Garth, the slinging of the schoolbag over my shoulder, the first few steps, and the steady trudge along the road; yet at each of these stages there was still a vestige of hope left; but when I reached the top of the hill and saw Kirkwall lying directly before me my last hope vanished, and I went down the slope as if my arms were bound and a warder were walking behind me. The sound of the school bell ringing as I loitered down Dundas Crescent seemed to be telling me for the last time to fly; but instead I ran as fast as I could toward it, knowing there was only that one road, which grew harder the nearer I approached its end. I have never managed to see St Magnus's Cathedral with an untroubled eye since then; a film of fear clings to it simply because it is associated with those mornings when I looked down on Kirkwall, where, hidden behind houses, stood the school.

from *An Autobiography* by Edwin Muir

Questions

1   What emotional experience is being described in this extract?
2   What comparison does Edwin Muir use to show his attitude towards school? What words and phrases support this idea?
3   What associations does St Magnus's Cathedral have for him as a result of his childhood experiences?

Practice work

1 Describe an experience from your childhood which had a strong emotional effect on you.

Picture

2 Look at the picture. Describe an experience from your childhood when you felt lost or lonely.

Remembering people

When you are describing people you remember from childhood, concentrate on conveying the personality of the character recalled. You need to supply great detail to bring out someone's special qualities.
Read the following extracts which describe two such unforgettable characters.

Mrs Battey

But Mrs Battey was a 'canny body', a good neighbour and a generous friend. She was a very large, florid, good-tempered excitable lady; she was almost stone deaf, and had a very penetrating voice the deaf often have. She screamed like a gaudy cockatoo when she laughed. She looked like one at times, as she waddled round our little backyard. She had a beaky nose and pince-nez – gold-rimmed glasses of which she was very proud; they shook and flashed when she let off her screams of laughter. Whenever she 'held forth', she showered her listeners with 'spit'. She had the first set of false teeth I ever saw, with bright orange gums. They were possibly too big for her: they protruded, and gave her smiles a brilliant, lopsided look; they kept dropping and slipping and clicking unexpectedly, in a manner which as a little boy I found interesting. She had a small silent husband who worked on the railway, and whom she always addressed in full: 'Mister Battey!' she would shout to him out of the upstairs window, or: 'Thomas Battey, I want you up here!' And poor Mr Battey, a burnt out Woodbine hanging on his lower lip, would trudge up and down the back stairs with pails of coal or buckets of water. I don't recollect anything more about her husband, except that he used to scrub the backyard in his bare feet with an enormous 'Corporation' street-broom. But Mrs Battey provides me with one of my most alarming childhood memories.

from *The Only Child* by James Kirkup

1 What sort of person was Mrs Battey?
2 What do we find out about Mrs Battey's physical appearance?
3 Why did Mrs Battey seem like a 'gaudy cockatoo'?
4 What does the description of Mr Battey's appearance and behaviour tell us about Mrs Battey's character?
5 What is it about Mrs Battey which provides James Kirkup with an 'alarming childhood' memory?

Samson

There was only one creature who constantly haunted the crossroads and he was called Samson. He actually lived on the Chowk*. Not above it, not two hundred yards away from it, not in the houses in the alleys behind it, but on the pavements outside the Kayani and Sachapir cafés. He had picked up his nickname because he had long, black hair down to his podgy shoulders. He must have had another perfectly good Parsee name, but 'Samson' was what we knew him as.

He was massive. Fat hung about his face, wrinkled and dangling like the jowls of a bulldog. Counting his chins was a competition on the Chowk. People said he ate three chickens at a go and five platefuls of rice a day. His belly hung over the tight cord of the white pyjamas he wore day and night. His shirt looked like a bedspread. He walked in the fashion which was popular with the people we called 'heroes', his arms stretched into stiff bows on either side of his body, legs wide and feet pointed outward. It was supposed to tell people who were watching that your muscles were so thick they prevented movement.

Samson would sit with Kolmi on the pavement outside the Kayani restaurant, waiting for betting slips or for the results of the cotton figures racked to be declared. He would be in and out of the restaurants. He hardly ever left the Chowk.

* the Chowk – a shopping area

He didn't bet, didn't smoke, didn't drink and never had a regular job. He earned some food by being the unofficial nightwatchman on the Chowk, paid by the owners of the Sachapir and the Kayani in cups of single char and platefuls of rice, which he'd eat when the cafés closed their doors and cleaned out their kitchens at two in the morning. The only work he ever got paid for was body-carrying. When a Parsee of our neighbourhood died, Samson would shroud himself in the white muslin coat and pyjamas of the khandias and help carry the corpse on a wooden bier through the town to the Towers of Silence on the hill beyond Golibar Maidan[**] where the community left its dead to be eaten by vultures.

Funerals were, of course, occasional employment. The fees he got for leading the team of shoulderers would pay his debts to the betel-nut wallahs and buy him the meat that charity wouldn't afford.

Late at night if I passed through the Chowk, I would see Samson laying out the bundle of blankets which the owners of the Kayani allowed him to keep in the corner behind the counter. His bed was one of the cement parapets outside the cafés.

'Still awake Samson?'

'Oh it's you, nalha. I'm just checking the locks on the Ahura Cycle Mart and Kaiko's Chemist's shop. Doctor Bharucha forgot to put the padlock on his dispensary today.'

There was the story of how he'd surprised two thieves breaking into the Ahura Cycle Mart one night. In his excitement he had mangled three bicycles instead of the thieves. There was also the story of how Samson had dealt with the Gurkha[***] who had presented himself in a smart khaki uniform to the shopkeepers of the Chowk and had been appointed by them as the official nightwatchman. The Gurkha, with his five foot wooden stick and reputation for bravery, had challenged Samson's right to loiter and sleep

[**] Maidan – a large field
[***] the Gurkha – a Nepalese soldier

107

in the Chowk and check the locks of the shops he had guarded for many a year.

'The pugnose is looking for trouble,' Samson had said.

The Gurkha had been found by the sweepers of the gutters below the bridge at the end of Sachapir Street one morning, alive but with a broken back, staunchly refusing to tell the police how his stick came to be in three pieces and how he had accidentally fallen from the bridge into the gutter.

from *Poona Company* by Farrukh Dhondy

Questions

1 What does the writer remember about Samson's appearance?
2 What jobs did Samson do? What do they suggest about him?
3 What was so unusual about the way he lived?
4 Why was he called Samson? What information in the passage shows that he was well named?
5 What impression does the writer give of Samson's character, which shows why he found him so memorable?

Practice work

Describe a character you remember from your own childhood. Try to convey the person's individuality. By describing physical appearance, way of speaking, behaviour and habits or mannerisms, show why the character is so memorable.

Choosing the style

One way of writing about your experiences is to relate the memories from **the point of view of an adult looking back at the past**. Your description can be distant and unemotional. In the following extract, the writer describes his childhood experiences in this way.

Washing Day

It was extraordinary how many of those conflicts with mother began with food. It was always a burning (not to say a baking) problem between us. The very first food trouble I recall was over a parcel of fresh herrings which had been left in the care of my elder brother and me in the kitchen while my mother went somewhere. Was I more than three? I rather doubt it. I have no idea where mother went. But remembering her zeal in helping neighbours I am sure she would not have left unfinished mangling, un-cooked herrings, a bathtub of clothes, and two mischievous small boys in the same room unless it had happened that Mrs Smalls, who had a lame back, had fallen downstairs, or Mrs Postlethwaite's vapourish adolescent daughter, who was too delicate to work, had another fit. But there it was – a pile of clothes still in their glistening suds, stood soaking in the zinc bath in which we, too, were scrubbed from time to time, and a great glorious mangle which clanked like a goods train going through a tunnel when you worked it, tempted our hands, and, peeping with pearly eye from newspapers they were wrapped in, were half a dozen shin-ing herrings. The first experiment we launched was to try to push wet clothes through the mangle just as mother did. Bobby turned the handle. He was my elder by two years, but in these things he did as he was told. All this proved excitingly easy with the small things like handkerchiefs and bibs and nappies, except for the trifling disadvantage that we forgot to put anything behind the mangle to catch them, and they fell on the floor and got dirty all over again. But that was the fate of clothes anyway. Sodden towels, however, proved more than we could manage, they were too heavy to lift, and the result of trying was that I got wetter than anything else in the room. All too soon the labour of mangling began to pall on us, and we turned our attention to the herrings which had never ceased to stare nosily at us from the bed of newspapers on the stove. Alas, fishes were not kittens. There was no way of playing with fishes except to make them swim, and no place for them to swim except in the wash tub, now sufficiently relieved of clothes to show a convenient expanse of soapy ocean. And here the herrings had to go. But they showed a mute disinclination to demonstrate their powers. They flopped into the bath and lay there, decorating the sodden clothes in a fashion I now recognise as surrealist, but which then seemed to me more or less normal, and not without its attractions except that the whole thing was too static to interest us long. Something had to be done, and the fishes were taken out again. Bobby and I knew from long observation that everything which came out of the wash tub went through the mangle, and through the mangle went the herrings, my brother vigorously turning the handle, while I pushed the fishes in by their tails. If you have never tried to push a fish by its tail you won't see the difficulty I was in. In the water the herrings were supine. On the mangling board they seemed to gather life of their own and flopped and wriggled against my pressures. In the end they had to be guided in, and in they went and so did my fingers. And mother returned from rescuing Mrs Smalls, or from putting a spoon between the teeth of Mrs Postlethwaite's daughter, to find the kitchen in uproar, blood and fish smeared over me, who was roaring from an injury more fancied than real, and my brother yelling, more from fear of the consequences than from any particular sympathy. We had woken up Muriel, who bellowed from the pram, a useful diversion, we hoped.

Order was restored with a speed which disconcerted even me. How was I to know that my mother could swoop with the dash and ferocity of a regiment of cavalry? It was granny who had the last word when she said with a gleam that she had always suspected I would come to a sticky end, and now was certain of it.

from *A Boy Down Kitchener Street* by Leslie Paul

1 How does the writer introduce this incident and how is it clear that this is an adult looking back?
2 What details does the writer leave out which would have been very important at the time to a three year old?
3 'But they showed a mute disinclination to demonstrate their powers.'
 What does the writer mean by this? How would the situation have appeared in the mind of a three year old?
4 Pick one part of the description where the writer could have developed the thoughts or feelings of a child and rewrite it as though you were the child.

Another method is to try and relive the experience **and write about it as though you were actually there**. This can turn the experience into an amusing incident as the next extracts shows.

Waking Up

I could hear the milkcart in the street. The horse, Bugger, stamped his feet irritably every time it had to stop. I knew the horse was called Bugger, because that's what the milkman called him.

'Hey, you Bugger. Give over ... Hold on a bit, Bugger ... Whoa, you Bugger.'

I lay in bed and could hear Bugger's iron-clad feet clipping the tarmac like four giant ice skates. Sometimes he snorted and the sound came to me like wind blowing in a chimney. The sounds of the milkurns were thin as tinsel for the empty ones and solid thick for the full ones. I lay abed, sharing with two brothers, and wouldn't open my eyes. I tried to make my ears tell me things. I made them pierce the bedroom walls and stand in the street to let me know if it was raining outside. They couldn't hear any sounds of rain but I mistrusted them. It *had* to rain today because I didn't want it to. I tried to make my ears read the sky for sounds of clouds, rainclouds, humping into each other like bullies in a playground. I tried to make my ears listen for the sizzling sound of sunlight, like bacon frizzling in a pan. My ears were liars because they told me nothing, and that's the biggest lie anybody or anything can tell. The lie of silence; which doesn't exist.

I didn't open my eyes. I stretched them. Stretched my eyelids. The dark purple of tight shut eyes gave way to warmer red. I held that colour and tried to examine it. Streaks of lighter colours painted across my lids, flower-colours. I stretched them a bit more and there was golden yellow, the colour of pollen sticking to a bumblebee's belly. I took a deep breath and opened my eyes. Sunlight snatched them towards the bedroom window, and the dazzle of blue sky brought me fully awake. I climbed out of bed and went to the window and it was a fête day of summer warmth and sunlight. It pleased me the same as pop does when it tingles bubbles at the back of your nose. It was a glorious day and not a threat of wet clouds anywhere. The narrow street was dusty with sunlight, so rich that even the dark shadows it couldn't reach took some heed of the sun-glow and mellowed into warm mahogany.

from *Summer's End* by Archie Hill

Questions

1 How do you know that Archie Hill is writing from the point of view of a child?
2 Pick out some of the comparisons which are very much those of a child. Are they effective?

Another style of writing which can make your memories lively and amusing is to use a **mocking one**. The following essay written by a pupil shows how this is done.

The Edinburgh Rock Affair

Now that I am 'grown up' and about to leave school, I have finally summoned up enough courage to admit to a terrible crime which I committed long ago.

At the tender age of four years, I entered school and settled down to enjoy this marvellous experience of being a schoolgirl. Being one of the 'big girls' that is, big in height, I was put in the yellow bands. My great friend, Ruth sat beside me and my cup of joy was full.

Every morning at half past ten, Miss Fraser, our teacher, announced break time, and then thankfully went to make her cup of tea. The milk-duty girl, puncher at the ready, attacked the bottle tops with glee, and the straw girl armed herself with the box of straws. Meanwhile, we ordinary mortals retrieved our play-pieces from our desk, and set out before us the morning's goodies. I believe, on the morning in question, that I had an egg sandwich, a piece of cake and two toffees – but, horror of horrors, one was nutty! This was a catastrophe! I hated nuts! As I gasped in consternation, Ruth stood up and went to fetch her milk. I felt too shocked to move. What was I to do? It was at this moment of greatest weakness that I espied an enormous, pink, crumbly, delicious piece of Edinburgh Rock. I have a secret passion for Edinburgh Rock. Ruth's mother had given her two pieces, one of which was at that precise moment being savoured by Ruth. The other lay before my eyes. I had only to stretch out my hand and it would be mine. The temptation was overpowering. However my principles would not allow me to steal. Instead I effected an exchange, my horrible, nutty concoction for Ruth's delightful confection. The switch was quickly done, and I went for my milk ecstatically munching my prize.

My joy was short-lived. Understandably Ruth was at a loss to know how her piece of Edinburgh Rock had been 'magicked' into a nutty toffee. She complained to Miss Fraser and the heinous crime was revealed. But what sinner had stooped so low? I shrank back beside the milk bottles. Have you ever tried to look like a milk bottle? It is impossible, believe me. However my red face was not my betrayer. Another yellow band girl, Elizabeth Anne Sneerwell, was unable to restrain herself from 'sneaking'. I have not forgiven her since. My guilt discovered, I had to face the disgust of my comrades. The humiliation of that moment will always haunt me. My punishment was no less severe. Miss Fraser ordered that my card of gold stars should be confiscated and that I must start another. All my lovely gold stars – so hard earned! Now I would never be top of the class!

In general, I am a fairly law-abiding soul, and so you may well understand that the memory of that day troubled me for a long time. I was convinced that, if it were brought to light again, I should never be made a school prefect. I therefore kept it quiet. Having since achieved my goal and joined the 'hierarchy', I felt obliged to make full confession of my sin. I ask your forgiveness.

Questions

1 Why does the writer call what she did a 'terrible crime'?
2 What does she mean by 'we ordinary mortals' and what does it show of the writer's attitude to school life?
3 Pick out and comment on three occasions when she deliberately exaggerates. What is the effect of these?

Practice work

Give an account of an incident from your childhood written in such a way that you mock your attitude, behaviour or thoughts at the time.

Organising the ideas

Ideas or memories need a structure. One way you can do this is to take a subject which shows the stages in your growing up. Here is an extract which illustrates this technique.

Books

But why about the age of nine, I began to bolt printed matter as if it were some precious nourishing substance I cannot imagine: apart from the Bible, the *Pilgrim's Progress*, *Gulliver's Travels* and a book by R M Ballantyne about Hudson Bay, the previous tenant of the farm had left in the loft over the kitchen a great jumble of weekly papers and old books. There were numbers of a paper called, I think, *The Christian World*, dating from several years back. They contained nothing but accounts of meetings and conferences, announcements of appointments to ministries, and obituary notices; yet I read them from beginning to end. There was also a thick volume bound in calf and containing verbatim report of a controversy between a Protestant divine and a Roman Catholic priest some time about the middle of the last century with a long argument on transubstantiation and many references to the Donai Bible which greatly puzzled me, for I did not know what the Donai Bible was. There was a novel all about young women, which I think now must have been *Sense and Sensibility*: I could make nothing of it, but this did not keep me from reading it. And the monthly parts of *The Scots Worthies*, which my father had carried with him from Sunday, and which were now in hopeless confusion, I went over carefully, arranging and repairing them, until the book assumed consecutive form. My father was so touched by this act of piety – for he regarded the book as almost a sacred one – that he had it handsomely bound in leather for me: a big tome of a thousand pages. All this passed through my mind; it was poor stuff without a vestige of nourishment, and it did not leave a trace behind. I read as if I were under some compulsion, as if my mind were crying for food and if there was none to be had must eat bran instead. I read all my school books as soon as I got them; I read *The People's Journal*, *The People's Friend* and *The Christian Herald*. I read a complete series of sentimental love tales very popular at the time, called '*Sunday Stories*'. I read a new periodical called *The Penny Magazine*, which my brother Willie got; it was modelled on *Tit-bits*, and contained all sorts of useless information. But I had no children's books and no fairy-tales; my father's witch stories made up for that.

A child's imagination is unbelievably vivid, and I do not know whether it was a benefit or a calamity when my brother Willie, out of pure kindness began taking *Chums* for me ... The line of *Chums* was adventure stories in savage lands. There was always a hero with a pointed beard, sailors with soft bushy beards and honest faces, and a boy called Frank. This small company passed through sunless canyons, forded alligator-infested rivers, cut their way through dense jungles and fought savage tribes set on by bad, white, clean-shaven men, meanwhile foiling the attacks of lions, tigers, bears and serpents. Returned to England with their riches, they dropped through trapdoors in rotting wharves and languished in dripping dungeons until the sailors, having broken out, returned like a benevolent music hall chorus to rescue the others, with a vast tattoo of sturdy fist on villainous faces. The excitement of following these adventures was more a pain than a pleasure and everything was so real to me that when I was herding the cows on the side of the hill I would often glance over my shoulder in case a tiger might be creeping up behind me. I knew with one part of my mind that there were no tigers in Orkney, but I could not resist that nervous backward jerk of the head.

I battened on this rubbish, some of it dull, some too exciting, until when I was eleven a school history book containing biographies of Sir Thomas Moore, Sir Philip Sidney and Sir John Eliot showed me that reading could be something quite different.

from *An Autobiography* by Edwin Muir

Questions

1 What does the writer use to structure his childhood memories?
2 Explain clearly the three major stages in his development which he describes.

Essay work

Choose one of the following essay questions. **Use the skills** you have learned so far to make sure your personal writing is vivid and interesting.

1 Write about a time when you were alone, describing the occasion and your feelings.

2 Write about a time when you had to settle in a new environment. Describe your thoughts and feelings about the difficulties you faced, and some of the people you met.

3 'I was never so disappointed in my life!' Write about your thoughts and feelings before, during and after an event which disappointed you a great deal.

4 Write about some of your daydreams and secret ambitions or special interests.

5 Write about the toys, games or pets you remember from your childhood.

6 'If a person admires you a lot you despise him and don't care – and it is the person who doesn't notice you that you are apt to admire.' Write about people you know who fit this description.

7 Read the extracts on page 118 from a diary written during the war. Write a few entries for your own diary covering an important time in your life. Choose different incidents or experiences to write about and describe your thoughts and feelings vividly.

Friday 31 May

The longest day ever! Every time the telephone rang one expected news. Mrs Carter came in at 10 am to say that she had heard through Major Cox that two days before our men of the 1/7th Battalion Royal Warwickshire Regiment were safe. We were so happy to hear this, but later, on ringing up one another, we found each had heard something of the kind and no one seemed to set great store by it. So our spirits went down and down and the day wore slowly on. We worked in the garden and lest we should not hear the telephone, we gave our big bell to Mrs Biggs at the telephone exchange next to us to ring for us while Kate was out. After supper a walk with Twink in an endeavour to calm and compose oneself in the tranquil fields so rich in their late spring growth.

Saturday 1 June

Still no news. The men are evacuated from Flanders via Dunkirk day by day and great are the deeds of the Navy and Air Force. Against fearful odds the men withdraw from their perilous position. Many more are able to get away than was at first thought possible. Grim stories are told. Their bravery is unexcelled. The land is flooded on either side of a wide passage to Dunkirk near the coast and, in spite of terrific bombardment, our men are coming through.

Picture 8 Use the picture opposite to describe a similar happy incident from your childhood.

Writing your opinions

There are two types of discussion essays: one in which you argue the case for and against a particular subject; the other, in which you simply express your own opinion. For both types of essays, you must be able to gather enough ideas on the subject, arrange those ideas so that the line of your argument is clear and express them in a lively and persuasive way. When you are gathering your ideas, consider whether there are any social, economic, political, moral or historical aspects to the question.

Gathering ideas

Read the extracts and headlines on pages 120–121. Jot down any ideas which you have on each subject.
Working in pairs, compare and discuss your lists.
Choose one of the topics, preferably one about which you have gathered most ideas.
Write out, in order of importance, a summary of each point you have made.
Compare your lists with another couple who have chosen the same subject, and discuss any points of agreement or disagreement.

BELT UP! ... that's the message from the Paris shows for this summer's fashion, says Retail Fashion Editor Jean. 'Belts are *in*, and not just the skinny little things of yesteryear but big, wide cummerbunds in suede, leather and fabrics.' It's not a fashion for fatties: 'They're designed to emphasise an hour-glass figure,' says Jean.

Fashion is one of this country's greatest sources of revenue, but as a major industry it receives less of the business interest and national investment that it needs.

Staying in tune with nature

It is difficult for the landscape of our reveries to live up to expectations. Too often the silence of an idyllic village is broken by the noise of container lorries, and views over meadows and woods are interrupted by outbreaks of architectural bad manners.

Wasting a whole future in front of our television sets

Sir, — Peter Fiddick asks, 'Is there such an urgent need for cable televison and its trimmings that four channels and satellite TV cannot satisfy?' (Arts Guardian, March 25) One must agree with his own reply, 'No'; TV already tempts us to waste too much valuable time.

A FINE MESS

But I had always assumed that tidiness, like growing old or being in a car smash, was something that happened only to other people.

In the morose swamp of despond into which this has plunged me, one cheerful bubble has surfaced. We spend all our time trying to be cleaner, sweeter, better looking, better organised than we are. And what happens if we succeed? Everyone hates us.

Developing an argument – for/against

When you are discussing the case for and against a particular subject you need to give both sides of the argument. Balance up the argument and decide which side you agree with. Present your view in a strong, persuasive way. Read the articles on the use of animals in experiments.

Brian Gunn
General Secretary
of the National
Anti-Vivisection
Society

Over 90,000 animals die every week in British laboratories, yet many researchers admit there are severe limitations in how effective the animal experimental method can be. Many people are in hospital as a direct result of adverse reactions to drugs thought to be safe for human use after extensive testing on many species of animals.

It is cowardly, inhumane and totally immoral to attempt to derive advantage from the infliction of pain and suffering on living animals. It's selfish too – if we were invaded by a species who thought themselves superior, would we consider that it was morally right for that species to experiment on *us?*

Legislation which permits experiments on living animals in Great Britain – the Cruelty to Animals Act – became law in 1876 and is still in force today. *It has never been amended.*

Animals are burnt, scalded, blinded, poisoned to death, exposed to radiation ... the obscene list is endless. The Act legalises cruelty in laboratories which, were you to commit against your pets, would incur severe punishment.

Research, of course, is essential, but there is always a right and a wrong way to conduct our search for knowledge. The National Anti-Vivisection Society, through its department, the Lord Dowding Fund For Humane Research, sponsors and promotes research aimed at the discovery of viable alternative techniques – like cell culture – which could replace living animals in cancer research and other areas. Countless animals are already being spared suffering as a result of using alternative methods.

Progress without hurting animals is indeed possible.

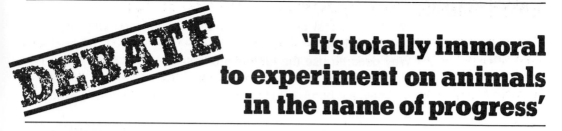

DEBATE

'It's totally immoral to experiment on animals in the name of progress'

**Lord Perry
of Walton**
*Chairman of the
Research Defence
Society and former
Vice-Chancellor of
the Open
University*

The virtual elimination of polio and diphtheria, the discovery of insulin in the treatment and control of diabetes, penicillins, drugs used in the treatment of high blood pressure ... these are just some of the benefits derived from experiments on animals.

That is why scientists believe that animal testing is necessary for the benefit of society and in most cases, there are no known satisfactory alternatives.

The fact is, a series of Acts have made animal testing compulsory. If drugs *weren't* tested on animals prior to their use by humans, people would say it's immoral to allow children to die as a result of taking untested drugs.

In 1876 the Cruelty to Animals Act was passed at a period similar to the present, when arguments for and against vivisection were arousing a high level of public interest and concern. As a result of that Act it was necessary for all experimental scientists carrying out research on animals to state the purpose of their experiments in order to obtain a Home Office licence to carry them out. But the important difference between 1876 and today is that a very much greater number of procedures are required before animal testing is carried out now. The government is committed to modernising the 1876 Act to take account of present day public feeling. The total number of experiments has fallen in recent years because of the increasing use of alternative methods, not requiring animals.

Scientists believe in the humane treatment of animals in their care, and in the need for proper legislation to ensure their welfare.

I'm confident that a large majority of people, given the facts, would agree that animal testing really is necessary for the benefit of society.

FOR

1   What is the first point made by Brian Gunn and why does he begin this way?

2   Why does he use the following phrases?
'cowardly, inhumane and totally immoral'
'Animals are burnt, scalded, blinded, poisoned to death, exposed to radiation . . .'

3   Is his example about invasion from another planet effective?

4   What criticism is he making about the 1876 Act?

5   What points does he make about alternative methods of research and how important is this to his argument?

AGAINST

1   Why does Lord Perry begin his argument in the way he does?

2   What does Lord Perry say to contradict Brian Gunn?

3   What extra information about the 1876 Act does he give and why does he give it?

4   What justifications are given for using animals in experiments?

5   How does he give weight to his argument in his final paragraph?

6   Which of these articles do you find most persuasive and why? Write the concluding paragraph for an essay on the use of animals in experiments. Sum up your own views in a powerful, persuasive way.

'Schools are establishments which waste the public's money and the pupils' time.'

Draw up two columns: FOR and AGAINST. Write the points which you would make on the above quotation in the appropriate column. Place the points in order according to their importance in the argument.

Now write an essay in which you discuss the case for and against the above quotation.

Structuring ideas

When planning your **argumentative essay** you can **structure your ideas – the points for; the points against** – with your own views as a conclusion. In a discussion or **opinion essay** you can **jot down the major points; arrange them in order of importance;** then conclude with a new angle on the issue or leave the reader with a question or thought.

> Read the following essay written by a pupil.

The Motor Car is the Curse of Modern Civilisation

The first economical motor car was produced by a man called Benz; it worked on the principle of the internal combustion engine using petrol as fuel. By the 1920s the motor car was available to the ordinary people though very few had one. Today in the 1980s nearly everyone has a motor car, some even have two or three. It seems then that the motor car is an essential part of modern civilisation which would break down without it.

The major use of the motor car is for travel, mainly for people to go to and from work. But it is also used by people for holidays and for transport on various trips. As a source of transport the motor car has to be used because the railways are too expensive and air travel is out of the question for most. If people did not have a car they could use whenever they wanted, relatives living far away could not be visited, people would have to find work in their home towns and 'getting away from it all' on Sunday would not be possible. So, a curse or not, the car is essential for the modern civilisation.

Because of the vast quantity of cars about today, complex road systems have to be built to carry the volume of traffic. These road systems often include motorways for easier long distance travel. The building of new motorways often comes up against a lot of opposition from those living in country areas because motorways spoil the scenery, despite landscaping. The roads in cities become congested

125

either because they are too small or they have too much traffic using them; this is a big problem with city roads. Roads in cities also take up a lot of land space which could otherwise be used for other things like factories or offices. So roads, an offspring from the motor car, are undesirable but necessary if we are to have the car.

Pollution is another major disadvantage of the car, but in recent years efforts have been made to reduce the amount of fumes a car gives out. The lead content of petrol fumes is poisonous and in an area where there is a lot of traffic it has been shown to affect the growth of small children. Petrol though at the moment is the only economical product that can be used to power a car, other methods such as paraffin or batteries are inefficient and expensive.

With an increase in the number of cars there has also been an increase in road accidents thousands of which occur each year, ranging from very minor accidents to fatal ones. Fatal accidents are caused by either a driver travelling too fast or being drunk. It is not surprising, therefore, that most accidents occur on motorways or in city areas. As long as there are cars, accidents will always happen because no driver can drive perfectly. So accidents also are a factor going against the car.

Many industries rely upon the motor car and roads. Haulage industries using heavy lorries have to use the roads and are the probable cause of their bad state of repair. Without the car and the vast road network, freight would have to be carried by the railways, which would have to be extended and even then roads would be necessary to carry freight from the terminals to the factory. So it seems at the moment industry could not survive without roads.

David Harper, aged 15

Questions

1 How does the writer 'twist' the essay title in the introduction?
2 What is the topic of each paragraph?
3 What changes would you make in the way he orders his ideas?
4 What is wrong with the ending?
5 Write a more suitable and effective conclusion to the essay.

Practice work

Write paragraph plans for the following essay titles. Think care-fully about the major points you want to make and the best order for them. Remember to have an unusual and powerful ending.

Money spent on defence would be better spent elsewhere
Sport is the curse of modern civilisation
Violent criminals – hanging is too good for them
Social class in Britain is a thing of the past

Expressing a view

You must try to express your ideas in such a way that the reader wants to listen to your views. To do this, you may adopt a humorous tone or an angry one. You can use quotations, examples or stories to illustrate a point and provide interest.

Read the following extracts and answer the questions.

Whose health is it anyway?

KATHARINE WHITEHORN

THE ANNUAL agony of getting rid of a few of the books that stand around in heaps on the floor has just been completed; and I'm interested to see that most of the ones I think I can do without are all books urging me to improve my health.

I suppose I must admit, grudgingly, that I have nothing against health as such. But I do find myself locking horns more and more often with a beast that is rapidly turning into a sacred cow: the need for preventative medicine. The argument generally goes like this. We spend a lot on health; we have a lot of advanced technical devices for curing people; would it not be better to stop them getting sick in the first place?

My first, perhaps minor, objection is that the cost statistics are phoney. Lung cancer, heart disease, accidents, the number of man-hours lost every year from low back pain – what it all costs can easily make your hair stand on end. But what no one can assess is what the cost would be if you *hadn't* crashed the bike, died of lung cancer or suffered the fatal heart attack – if you live on, to that which should accompany old age, as strokes, arthritis, hip replacement and a good 10 years in a geriatric home.

If you take your body to the doctor, it is like taking a car to the garage: you say, there's a terrible knocking under the bonnet, could you do something about it? Either he can or he can't – and of course, he may tell you to stop driving with so little oil (if a garage) or so much alcohol (if a doctor). The point is that you, the patient, have asked him to do something about your physical state. And insofar as prevention means simply anticipating a physical ailment and stopping it before it has got started – with things like vaccination or inoculating you against diphtheria or malaria – I'm all for it.

But the current urge is towards a prevention of illness which involves the lifestyle.

High blood pressure is controllable by an altered lifestyle and a regime of pill-taking (among other things), but a young man has surely the right not to turn himself into a young hypochondriac for fear of what might happen when he's fifty. Dentists keep telling you you'd have much better teeth if you cleaned them five times a day; but I might decide I was not put into this world to spend my entire time brushing my teeth.

Don't get me wrong; I am all in favour of any action, by government or anyone else, that stops anyone making *other people* ill – illnesses caused by putting them to work with dry asbestos, or allowing lead to pour out of cars into homes along the highway, or tipping industrial waste into the water, or advertising. But I never elected anyone to the right to make me healthy myself; or the moral right to make me feel that my unhealthy habits are a sin against the religion of medicine.

Questions

1 How does the writer introduce the subject? What seems to be her attitude to it right from the start?

2 What does she say is the basic argument in favour of preventative medicine? What is her attitude to it?

3 What points does she make about cost statistics? How does she illustrate her points?

4 With what aspects of preventative medicine does she agree?

5 What is her main objection to preventative medicine? How does she convey her opinion?

FEAR AND BRITAIN'S INDIANS

Festivals are fun, but don't cure street violence

OPINION

THE FESTIVAL of India has at last happened after much planning and discussion. There is a feeling of achievement. Mrs Gandhi came all the way from India to attend the opening and Mrs Thatcher was generous in devoting her time to help launch the festival. For six months people will be able to see beautiful exhibitions and recitals of Indian music and dance.

When I joined the Festival of India Committee I hoped the festival would give an opportunity to analyse what has happened to the culture of Indians living here, related to India's present and past. The involvement of the Indian community with its artists, writers and creative people could have given the festival a real sense of participation. But an Arts Council official closely associated with the festival's organisation dismissed my suggestion. 'We want a festival, not a carnival.' However, the Indian community *is* organising its own varied events although with little financial help and support.

The major part of the festival takes place in central London. Travelling is so expensive that I wonder how many of Britain's Indian community can afford to visit it. Nor will it reach the majority of the British working class who tend not to visit museums and art galleries and yet it is essential to help to bring a change in their attitude to India and Indians.

The festival has a special meaning for me because I live here. I came as a young student and my development as a painter and writer took place in this country. While studying town planning in Leeds in 1962 I experienced racial discrimination for the first time. 'How black are you?' people asked me on the telephone when I was looking for a room.

But suddenly the atmosphere changed when Enoch Powell delivered his 'rivers of blood' speech. As politicians introduced bills to restrict immigration and debated about the presence of coloured immigrants, people started expressing their views openly. I faced abuse in the streets, which disturbed me.

On the night of the 1974 general election I was returning home after spending a happy evening with friends in Chelsea. A group of young people followed me from Wapping Underground station along the deserted streets, taunting and insulting me. As I was about to enter my building I was attacked and left lying unconscious on the pavement. It was a traumatic experience and I have not yet recovered. I felt so frightened that I had to leave the East End. My inner ears are permanently damaged and I have frequent attacks of dizziness.

As I sit in my studio in Pimlico reflecting on the festival, another incident keeps haunting me. On the evening of the inaugural concert I arrived early to help a group of children from a multi-racial primary school in Inner London perform an improvised animal dance in front of the Festival Hall. It was part of the Alternative Festival. A middle-aged, well-dressed Englishman came up to me, raised his arm in salute, said 'National Front' and walked on.

When I mingle with the dignitaries at festival receptions I am treated as an artist and writer. But when I am walking alone in the streets of London I am made to feel I am just an Indian who is not wanted. The colour of my skin makes me vulnerable.

I believe in creating understanding between people through art and culture and I am glad the festival is taking place. But for me the Festival of India will only be a success if it helps to remove the fear I experience daily and share with many other Indians living here. I do not think it will and that makes me sad.

Questions

1 What seems to be the writer's opinion of the Festival of India at the start?
2 When and how does his attitude change?
3 What criticisms does he make of the festival's organisation?
4 What points is he making through the personal experience he relates?
5 What note does he end on? How effective is it as the conclusion of his opinions?

Essay work

Choose one of the following questions. **Use the skills** you have learned in this section to answer the question fully.

1 Read the following letter. Write an essay giving your views on the changing role of men and women.

A Question of Priority

I read with interest Jane Root's excellent article No Jobs For The Girls (February). I am not anti-feminist. But given that unemployment is bad anyway, surely it is better for a man to have a job than a woman?

If a woman feels demeaned by full-time housework, it is easy to understand the man who says that he wouldn't do any extra housework in case it turned him into 'a namby-pamby not fit for any job'. After all, men have had centuries of conditioning to be the strong sex, the breadwinners. They can't be expected to change overnight.

And men are still more likely to have dependants, more likely to be expected to pay out for other people. Exceptions could and should be made for women left alone with a young child or an aged parent.

I don't agree either that people think any better of the "mean or stupid" than the unemployed just because of their "fat wallets". Most of us are too near the edge ourselves, and are hoping for considerate treatment if we too should topple and become yet another statistic.

It is wrong for any person who feels the need to work to be idle. However, we should try to keep things in perspective. Women have their work cut out caring for people – from the youngest to the oldest. Why should they feel they have to go out to work as well?

Unless she is a youngster leaving school and anxious to support herself perhaps a woman, on finding herself jobless, should retire gracefully to the background. Here she may be a tower of strength to others.

A Scotcher, Kenilworth, Warks.

2 Discuss the advantages and/or disadvantages of being 'one of the gang' or 'the odd man out'.

3   'When a man gives himself up to the government of a ruling passion – farewell cool reason and fair discretion.'
Discuss some particular interest of your own which has amounted to an obsession.

4   'The twentieth century may not be a very good thing but it's the only century we've got.'   Norman St John-Stevas

Write an essay giving your views on life in the twentieth century.

5   'I like to be frightened when I see a film. Not to upset people would be an obscenity.'   Roman Polanski

Give your views on violence in films and novels.

6   'To win your battle in this society, you've got to have your cave. Then food. Then some kind of mate. After that, everything's a luxury.'   Rod Steiger

Express your views on the important things in life, and the luxuries.

5 Formal writing

In formal writing (writing reports, accounts or letters), you need to give accurate and detailed factual information in a clear and concise way. The ideas must be developed and explained fully. Choose the most suitable form and tone in which to present the information.

Giving the facts

Factual details are important in making the information clear. Read the following information about the village of Laugharne.

Laugharne

Laugharne's name – pronounced 'Larn' – is inextricably linked with that of Dylan Thomas, the Swansea born poet who lived there 'off and on, up and down, high and dry', from 1951 until his tragically early death in America 16 years later aged 39.

The road from St Clears runs down to the village through a landscape of low, rolling hills. From the brow above St Martin's Church where the poet was brought home from New York for burial, there are views over the broad waters of Carmarthen Bay to the distant hills of the Gower. The oldest parts of the church date from the thirteenth century, but it was built about 1350 by St Guy de Brian, Edward III's standard bearer at Crécy, and restored in 1873. The interior is notable for its Victorian stained glass, and for walls crammed with commemorative tablets. Several recall members of the seafaring Laugharne family, including Vice-Admiral John Laugharne who died in 1819. Dylan's grave is marked by a simple white cross made of wood in a new part of the graveyard.

Several elegant Georgian buildings – one of which, near the post office was Dylan's parents' home – and numerous attractive cottages line the eighteenth-century Town Hall with its white tower, belfry and weather cock. The tower looks down Duncan Street. *Brown's Hotel*, a block away from the Town Hall, was a favourite haunt of the poet. His other 'locals' included the black-and-white *Corporation Arms* at the foot of Gosport Street, and the pink-washed *Cross House Inn*. Gosport Street and Wogan Street, which starts near the gateway to Castle House, slope down to The Grist, a shop-flanked square on the site of a monastery. One side opens out on to the shore, where small boats moor beneath the lofty walls of the ruined Laugharne Castle. Henry II was entertained there on his way home from Ireland in 1172, and the castle is believed to have been destroyed by Llewelyn the Great's army in 1215. In the sixteenth century it was repaired and altered by Sir John Perrott – generally acknowledged as an illegitimate son of Henry VIII – and was later held by both Royalists and Roundheads during the Civil War.

Questions

1 What facts are given about Laugharne's geographical position?
2 What are you told about the buildings in the village?
3 What is the historical importance of the place?
4 What connection does Dylan Thomas have with the village?
5 Does this passage give you a clear impression of Laugharne? If not, what type of information do you think needs to be included.

Practice work

1 Here are some facts about Telford, in Shropshire. Read them carefully.

Telford

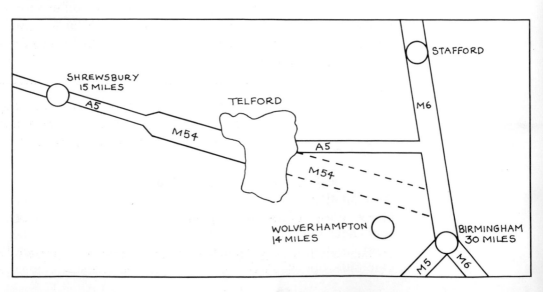

– M54 runs through the town – links with National Motorway network – 50 minutes to Birmingham – international airport facilities for passenger and freight – three major industrial areas for development – will provide jobs.

Housing areas adjoining lakes and woodlands – restored cottages and new estates – gold medal for design – reasonable rents and prices – schools and health centres close by. Covered heated shopping centre – major stores and hypermarkets – easy access by public transport – thousands of car parking spaces.

Sports and leisure centres for squash, badminton, swimming, judo etc. – artificial ski slope – championship length Hay Golf course – amateur soccer leagues – Shropshire minor county's cricket club – athletics club.

Ironbridge nearby – Iron Bridge itself spans the Severn Gorge – museums include Coalport for china, Coalbrookdale for iron and the remains of Abraham Darby's first blast furnaces – Blists Hill open air museum – Severn Valley Railway first authorised in 1853 ran through the Ironbridge Gorge – only Shrewsbury/Wolverhampton route remains open to passengers – restoration of steam locomotives at Horsehay.

2   You have been asked to write the introduction to the new edition of the Town Guide. Using the information given, write the introduction in such a way as to give a general impression of the kind of town Telford is.

3   Imagine you are one of the following:
an industrialist
a married man with two children
a tourist
Having read the facts about Telford, write a lengthy explanation of why you would want to go there.

137

Read the following information on how to get started at skiing.

- **Wear a padded, waterproof jacket with lots of roomy pockets, and long sleeves.**

- **Take a vest and a pair of thick tights or long johns, one or two polo-necked cotton sweaters, a thin and a thick jumper, and a pair of proper ski socks.**

- **A woolly hat is essential, as are special ski gloves or mittens that are close-fitting at the wrist.**

If you want to learn some basic movements, write to the Ski Club of Great Britain, address below. For 30p plus sae they'll send a list of artificial slopes in Britain.

Ski boots must be comfortable. Try them on in your ski socks: when you stand on your toes your feet shouldn't slip forward and you shouldn't be able to raise your heel more than 1.3 cm ($\frac{1}{2}$ in) inside the boot.

Skis, when upended, should reach to about your eyebrows, unless you're learning with Ski Evolutif, when you'll graduate from short skis to long ones.

Check sticks are the right length, too. Turn each upside down and hold it under the basket (which stops the pole sinking into the snow). Your elbow should be at the right angle.

Skiers uphill must avoid skiers lower down.

Fast skiers must avoid slower ones.

Don't show off by skiing faster than the grade of run you're on allows.

Don't ski through a class of pupils – if you have to stop on the piste (the prepared ski-run) get out of the way quickly.

You can ski without leaving Britain, but it won't necessarily be cheaper. Send for 'Ski Holidays in Scotland', from the Scottish Tourist Board, 23 Ravelston Terrace, Edinburgh EH4 3EU.
When choosing a resort on the Continent, look for good slopes and beginners' facilities, plus an English-speaking ski school. Head for the modern French resorts of Les Arcs, Flaine, Avoriaz, La Plagne or Isola 2,000 if you'd like to try the new Ski Evolutif method on short skis. It has a good record of helping beginners make fast progress. Cut down costs with self-catering apartments and coach travel.

1   For each paragraph write a few words which sum up the type of information given. From the information given, which do you think are the most important facts for a beginner to know? Give reasons for your choice. Are there any other pieces of information you think a beginner would need to know about skiing, which are not included here?

2   Choose a hobby you have or a sport you play and write a beginners' guide to it. Think about all the facts you will need to give. Set it out like the guide to skiing and add illustrations if necessary.

Expressing ideas concisely

When you are writing a report, article or letter you must express your ideas clearly so that the facts are fully understood.

> Read the following eye witness's report of a robbery, and the accurate account of the same accident.

I'd just finished giving my youngest his dinner and was at the gate waving goodbye to him as he went back to school. So let me see, it must have been about 12.45 when this van pulled up along the road and this bloke jumped out.

He ran into the house three doors away - you know the detached one with the flaky paint. There was another long-haired bloke skulking in the front seat. I thought they looked a bit suspicious but I didn't like to pry. About half an hour later I heard some loud bangs and I ran out in front to see this bloke jumping into the truck. It had to be at least half an hour because I always take my time cleaning up after lunch. Anyway, they drove off at a frightening speed. Me and a couple of other neighbours ran along to Mr Jiwan's place but we couldn't get any reply so we 'phoned the police. I can't remember the registration number. Mind you, I'm hopeless at figures.

Fifty armed police last night laid siege to a council flat after a retired Asian businessman who had advertised gold for sale was shot dead.

The siege, in Exford Drive, Bitterne, Southampton, ended after five hours when a man opened the door of the flat and surrendered.

Earlier 57 year old Mr Ebrahim Jiwan had been shot dead in his semi-detached house in nearby Dimon Hill, Bitterne Park.

Mr Jiwan, a Ugandan Asian who escaped the brutal regime of Idi Amin, had recently advertised locally that he had gold for sale.

He, his wife Maleksultan, 54, and their daughter Shamira were planning to emigrate to Canada in six weeks' time and had put their £25,000 house up for sale.

At 1.20 pm yesterday a car pulled up outside the house. A man went inside, leaving a woman at the wheel of the car.

Mr Jiwan, who had two other daughters and a son, was shot dead in the lounge of his home.

The killer left with a box of gold and another one containing jewellery after battering Mr Jiwan's wife over the head.

Police chased the car to the block of flats after a neighbour of the Jiwans gave them the number of the vehicle.

As police surrounded the building the woman who had been in the car – and did not go into the flat – phoned the police.

The gunman eventually agreed to come out of the flat after talking to police.

Last night a man and a woman were helping police inquiries – most of the gold and jewellery had been recovered.

Questions

1 What information given by the witness does not correspond with that given in the newspaper account?

2 What information does the witness give which is irrelevant?

3 What kind of vital information does she leave out?

4 What is wrong with the way the witness gives her account?

5 Rewrite the witness's statement as it should have been written.

Imagine you witness the incident described in this newspaper report. Write a clear, accurate account of what happened.

David Austin Cookson, aged 23, of Atley Crescent, Highfields, Stafford, admitted inflicting grievous bodily harm on 19 year old David Williams. He also admitted assaulting policemen Peter Edwards and Nicholas Jones, occasioning actual bodily harm.

Neil Williams, aged 22, of Binyon Court, Highfields, admitted assault occasioning actual bodily harm on a third policeman, Christopher Reynolds and was jailed for three months at Stafford Crown Court yesterday.

Mr David Gittins, prosecuting, said Cookson struck David Williams in the face at least three times with a beer glass which did not break and butted him in the head, in the Malt and Hops, Stafford, on New Year's Eve.

He said it was an 'unprovoked and extremely vicious' attack.

Officers Edwards and Jones were in the pub at the time and the assault against them happened outside, said Mr Gittins.

Officer Reynolds was called to the scene in a police van and Neil Williams assaulted him outside the pub, he said.

Mr Gittins said that inside the pub Neil Williams tried to restrain Cookson.

Read this information on buying a stereo system.

If you're considering buying your own sound system, the first thing to do is to decide how much money you can spend. The basic components should be the best you can afford right now; you can always add to your system or exchange one part for something of better quality in the future.

You should spend most money on the source of your sound: the turntable for records, a cassette deck for tapes, or perhaps a tuner for the radio. With the majority of first time buyers, the turntable will be the source, and many people will add a cassette player when they can afford it.

Always listen to your potential purchase before parting with your money. Take your time and don't let yourself be pressurised into buying anything.

Hal Lindes, guitarist with Dire Straits, has some good points for those buying their first system, with a budget of £200. As Hal says, it isn't essential to buy brand new equipment first time around, except for speakers, which could have been misused.

He suggests buying a good second hand amplifier for about £50. Look through the hi-fi magazines and stick to well-known makes.

When buying a turntable, remember that the stylus provided is probably quite cheap. When you can afford it, you can upgrade the stylus and produce a far superior sound. You may want to pay up to £70 to replace the existing model.

Questions

1   Sum up the advice given on what to do when buying a stereo system. Number each point, and put each one on a new line.

2   Make a list of the points Hal Lindes makes for those buying their first equipment.

3   Are there any points made in this article which are unclear? If so, explain why.

Practice work

Choose an item which you know well. Write a report providing useful information on what to look for when buying it.

Developing ideas

Some factual information needs developing and explaining for it to be clearly and completely understood. Statistical tables are like this. They present factual information in a numerical form. They have a special layout. All tables have a title which tells you the subject matter. They have rows (read across) and columns (read down) of facts and figures. Each figure can be understood by reading off what row and column it is in. What units the numbers represent is given at the top right hand side of the table. Footnotes at the bottom of the table may give further information and definitions.

Look at the statistical table opposite which tells you how people spend their leisure time.

1 What social and cultural activities are popular with all social groups?

2 What activities are most popular with the following groups?
professional
intermediate
skilled manual
semi-skilled

Write a paragraph on both of the following groups describing what they do with their leisure time. Explain what you think are the reasons for each group's preferences.
professional, employers and managers
semi-skilled and unskilled manual workers

Participation in selected social and cultural activities: by socio-economic group and sex, 1980

Annual average percentages

	Men			
	Professional, employers and managers	Intermediate and junior non-manual	Skilled manual	Semi-skilled and unskilled
Percentages in each group engaging in each activity in the 4 weeks before interview				
Open air outings				
Seaside	9	8	6	5
Country	7	5	4	2
Parks	4	4	3	3
Entertainment, social, and cultural activities				
Going to the cinema	10	13	10	8
Visiting historic buildings	15	12	7	4
Going to the theatre/opera/ballet	9	5	2	1
Going to museums/art galleries	5	5	2	2
Amateur music/drama	5	6	3	2
Attending leisure classes	2	2	—	—
Going to fairs/amusement arcades	2	2	2	2
Going out for a meal[2]	60	47	35	25
Going out for a drink[2]	61	63	68	63
Dancing	12	11	·14	10
Home-based activities				
Listening to records/tapes[2]	69	69	64	57
Gardening[2]	62	54	47	41
Games of skill	21	21	20	17
Needlework/knitting[2]	2	3	2	2
House repairs/DIY[2]	64	58	55	40
Hobbies	12	15	10	7
Reading books[2]	67	65	43	39
Total sample size (= 100%) (numbers)	2,089	1,717	4,107	2,093

Source: General Household Survey, 1980

145

Practice work

Pictures

The following pictures give advice to pedal cyclists on how to behave on the roads.

Do *not* carry a passenger on your cycle.

Do *not* carry anything in your hands or on the handlebars or crossbar of your cycle.

Do *not* hold on to a moving vehicle.

Always look behind you when starting off and stopping.

Do *not* hold onto another cyclist.

Do *not* ride too close behind a moving vehicle.

Using the information given in these pictures, write an article giving advice to cyclists on how to behave on the roads. Explain each point fully.

Organising ideas

You can present facts and information in a number of ways. You must choose the one most suitable for the subject you are dealing with. It is important that the facts are organised in a sensible order.

Read the following information for tennis teams which is written as **a memo**.

Memo

To	All members of the tennis teams
From	Head of PE
Date	
Subject	The County Tennis Tournament

The County Tennis Tournament will take place on Saturday 12 June at Chasely High School from 10.30 till approximately 6.00 p.m.

The coach will leave the school car park at 9.00 prompt. On arrival at Chasely High, make your way to the appropriate changing areas for your age-group. All competitors should have changed, signed in at the registration desk and be ready to start by 10.15 a.m.

Lunch is from 12.30 p.m. till 1.30 p.m. You should bring your own packed lunch but drinks will be provided.

The afternoon session commences at 1.30 p.m. When competitors have finished playing they may spectate or use the swimming pool. All pupils must be at the coach by 6.30 p.m.

The coach will return to school at approximately 7.15 p.m.

Questions

1 What is the nature of the information on this memo?
2 How has the information been ordered?
3 Why is it appropriate for the information to be organised in this way?

Practice work

Imagine you are in charge of organising a trip or event for your school. Write out the information for the people involved, using the same method of organisation as the memo.

Read the following report of a meeting, which has been organised as **the minutes**.

Report of the Meeting of the Village Dramatic Society

The meeting took place on the 22 April, in the Village Hall and was attended by all members of the committee. The Chairman, Mr Peters, read the minutes of the last meeting then proceeded to the first item on the agenda – the replacement of the leading lady, Miss Appleby.

Several names were put forward for discussion, but finally it was unanimously accepted that Mrs Pugh was the only person who would fit Miss Appleby's costume.

Mrs Jackson and Mrs Cook were asked to report on the present position regarding costumes. There was some difficulty in obtaining suitable silk for the Japanese kimonos but a contact had been found. The major problem was cast. Mr Jackson requested extra finance and Mr Whitehouse agreed to look into the possibility of allocating more money for costumes.

Mr Clarke reported that ticket sales were going well and that more tickets could be sold for Friday and Saturday if extra rows of seats could be fitted in. Mrs Andrews offered chairs from the school hall and Reverend Blake agreed to look into the possibility of fitting in the extra rows. Mr Peters pointed out the need to keep within fire regulations.

Mrs Allan reported some problems as regards catering – on one evening, the Guides needed the tea urn, and as yet the Grocery Store had not offered its usual donation of sugar and tea. Mr Peters agreed to make tactful enquiries into the matter of the tea and sugar, and Mrs Andrews offered to request the staffroom urn from the school.

A collection was made for a present for Miss Appleby and Mr Peters suggested recording the show to take to her in hospital.

The next meeting was arranged for the 28 April, and the meeting was declared closed.

Questions

1   In a few words, sum up the points for discussion as they might have appeared on the agenda for the meeting.
2   Why do you think they are arranged in this particular order?

Practice work Read the following information carefully.

East Lane Social Club
- Annual General Meeting - Friday 10th
                            December - 8.00pm
Chairman - Mr. Levine
Secretary - Mrs. Jessell
Read apologies from ??? and minutes.

AGENDA

1. Treasurer's report (Mr Patel) - good year - same profits even after major repairs to roof of club. - large expenditures - Christmas Party, Old Folk's Concert, new bar stools (good quality, last longer!)

2. Rules of entry to club -
proposition to insist on ties/jackets -
some discussion - little support -
majority stressed casual atmosphere.
What about family membership? (Mrs O'Reilly) Agreed - good idea - arrange cost next meeting.

3. Youth Club—
still noise and vandalism (local
residents)—

Invite leaders to next meeting ✓✓✓

4. Old folk's concert — great success —
should repeat.
Vote of thanks to all who helped (Get names
etc. later) N.B.

5. Cost of beer — discussion — mixed views → Go up!
Too cheap.
No profit.
Stay! Good for
trade.
Aim of club.
Close vote "Go uppers" won !!.
6. Next Meeting — 27th January (committee)

— 15th June — full meeting to
discuss Summer
outings.

Closed !

You are going to write the minutes for the meeting. Decide upon
the correct order for the information. Then write the minutes up
properly in complete sentences.

Read the following information for competitors taking part in the Birmingham Marathon, **arranged in numbered points.**

Information for Competitors and Friends

1   Car park A is at the Chelmsley Wood Shopping Area (free of charge) and is for male runners nos 11–2,200
     Car park B is at Schools in Gressel Lane (free of charge) and is for male runners nos 2,201–4,450 (Sir Wilfred Martineau and Byng Kenrick Schools). After changing you will be transported to the Registration Tent. (Please ensure that you arrive in time to register before 11 o'clock.)

2   The car park at the North Solihull Sports Centre (access from Cooks Lane) is for all ladies nos 4,414–4,750.

3   Please note *NO* cars or bikes will be allowed around the course, as most roads will be closed to all traffic, except for officials and the buses. The Police will stop anyone else.

4   Report to Registration before 11 o'clock and collect your plastic carrier bag containing: one number (attach to front of vest), large plastic bag with your number on for track suit etc. at the start of the event (this will be placed in numerical order at finish), a programme, a commemorative running vest and a questionnaire sheet.

5   All runners are to report to the starting area at 11.40 am and should go to the appropriate time zones, i.e. sub 2.45, 2.45–3.00 hrs, 3.00 hrs–3.30 hrs, 3.30 hrs–4.00 hrs etc.,

6   After the event, transport will take you back to the area where your car is parked or changing accommodation.

7   Refreshments will be available from the Registration Area from 10.00 am onwards.

Questions

1   What kind of information does this provide for the competitors?
2   Why is this the most suitable way of organising it?
3   How does the map help in presenting the information?

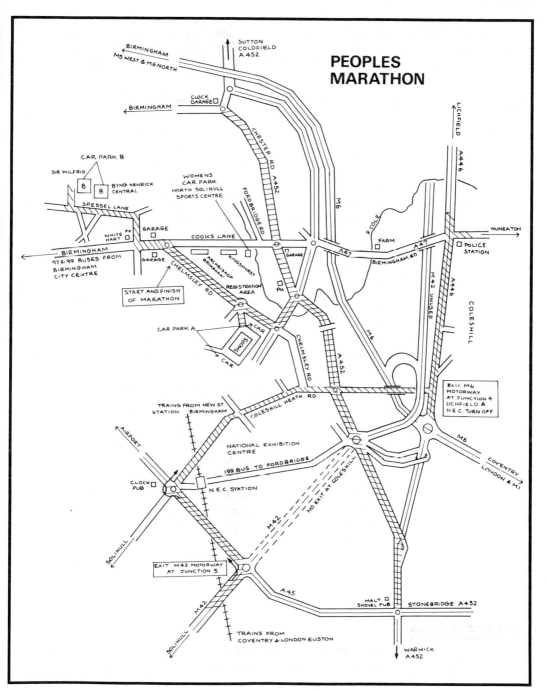

Practice work   A group of pupils from your school intends to visit the Annual Show and you have been asked to arrange the visit. Study the programme and the plan of the show. Write a report about the special attractions of the show for the group. Include in it suggestions about possible meeting places and a timetable for the visit so that you might cater for different interests.

The Annual Show

Afternoons 2–5.30
PROGRAMME
1.45–2.00 Opening ceremony
             Brass band

2.00–5.00   Horse competition
             (Presentation to winners 5.15)

2.00–4.00   Pets and Flowers Competition
             (Presentation to winners 4.15)

2.00–3.00   Disco competition
             Main arena

3.00–4.00   Fashion Show ending in
4.00–4.15   Fancy Dress Competition
             Main arena

4.15–5.15   Police Display
             Main arena

Open all day   Fair
               Shooting range
               Vintage car exhibition
               Restaurant/refreshment bars
               Craft stalls

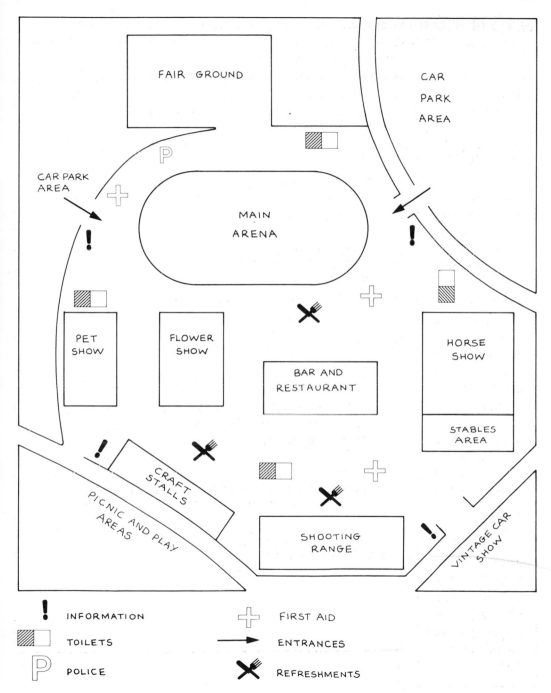

When **writing a formal or business letter** you must set it out correctly.
Read the following letter carefully.

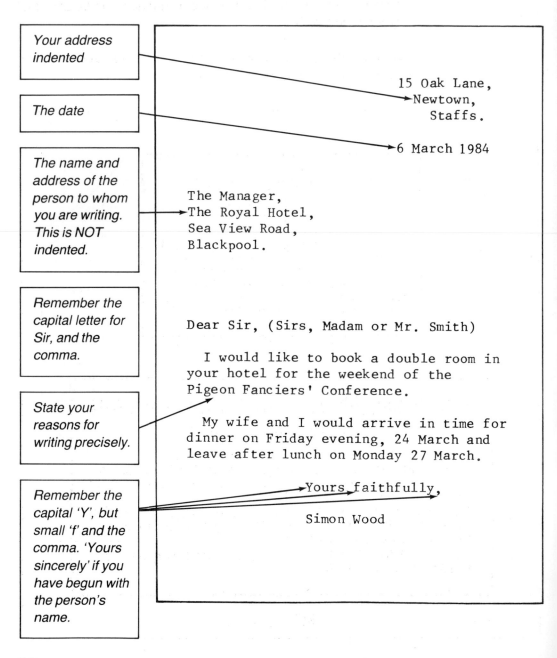

Your address indented	15 Oak Lane, Newtown, Staffs.
The date	6 March 1984
The name and address of the person to whom you are writing. This is NOT indented.	The Manager, The Royal Hotel, Sea View Road, Blackpool.
Remember the capital letter for Sir, and the comma.	Dear Sir, (Sirs, Madam or Mr. Smith)
State your reasons for writing precisely.	I would like to book a double room in your hotel for the weekend of the Pigeon Fanciers' Conference. My wife and I would arrive in time for dinner on Friday evening, 24 March and leave after lunch on Monday 27 March.
Remember the capital 'Y', but small 'f' and the comma. 'Yours sincerely' if you have begun with the person's name.	Yours faithfully, Simon Wood

Practice work Choose one of the following and write a suitable letter.

Write a letter making a booking for a dinner dance to be attended by your local club.

Write a letter giving details of your planned route and asking for suitable accommodation to be arranged.

Factual information can be presented in the form of **a newspaper or magazine article**. Read these two articles describing a fire at a chemical plant.

CHEMICAL BLAZE PROMPTS INQUIRY

By Gareth Parry

An MP has called for an inquiry into the fire at a chemical factory near Stalybridge, Greater Manchester, which resulted in 200 people being evacuated as storage drums exploded. It emerged yesterday that the local council had already ordered 40-gallon drums to be moved away from nearby houses.

The firm appealed against the enforcement order, and the Secretary for the Environment decided after a public inquiry last June, to give the firm until December to move the drums. Tameside Borough Council had originally decreed that the work should have been completed nine months ago.

One man died and another worker was seriously injured when the explosion at the Chemstar plant rocked the village of Carrbrook just before midnight on Sunday. The factory recycles solvents.

The dead man was Mr Michael McGrady, aged 40, of Little Lever, Bolton. He was unloading his lorry at the factory which employs 17 people.

Health and Safety Executive inspectors, who last month investigated a fire at a chemical warehouse at Wallington in Surrey during which 500 people were evacuated in the middle of the night, began their inquiries at the Chemstar plant yesterday. Mr Tom

Pendry, Labour MP for Stalybridge and Hyde, whose constituency includes parts of the hillside site, demanded an inquiry led by a senior person.

Local people have been concerned about the chemical drums, particularly when the chemical firm took over a building which had previously been used by a printer. They asked whether planning permission had been sought, but were told that once the site had been allocated for 'general industrial use' there was no need for any other permission to be sought.

Thousands of firms own factories and warehouses in Britain with chemical stores

INTO SAFETY

close by or in the middle of large centres of population, but no one officially knows where they are.

The Health and Safety Executive wants to introduce regulations forcing firms using or storing dangerous chemicals in large quantities to identify themselves. The regulations were drawn up four years ago but their introduction has met strong opposition from industry and has also been hampered by complicated EEC counter-proposals and directives.

As the 200 villagers of Carrbrook returned to their homes yesterday, the injured man, a process worker Mr Norman Halsall, was said to be seriously ill in hospital.

As 200 firemen damped down the ruins, Mr Pendry said that in 1977 the Health and Safety Executive, which deals with factory safety regulations, had assured local residents that there would be no risk to adjacent property. 'If it had not been for the vigilance of the fire service and if there had been a wind last night instead of dead calm, there could have been a terrible tragedy,' he said.

Mr George Molyneaux, Chemstar's managing director, said that there was a public inquiry a few weeks ago to consider a new installation at the plant. 'We were told to clear the site of drums by December 31. This was being done. We were told to do this because of a loading and access problem.'

Mr Molyneaux, who said he expected the plant to eventually reopen, said: 'We take all the precautions that are expected of us. The requirements of the factory inspectorate and insurance were satisfied.' Deputy Fire Officer Don Liddel said firemen received slight injuries. 'At one stage we had to deal with two rivers of blazing chemicals running down the road,' he said. Local people were told not to use water because of pollution risks.

from *The Guardian*

AFTERMATH OF

Drums exploded

Angry villagers demanded an inquiry last night into the massive chemical plant explosion which threatened to destroy their homes.

They accused Government officials of ignoring their warnings of a holocaust. And they vowed to fight bitterly to prevent the reopening of the factory, which recycles petrol-based chemicals.

The blast, which killed a driver and turned a process worker into a human fireball, hit the Chemstar plant, in Carrbrook, near Manchester, just before midnight on Sunday.

Police ordered 300 homes to be evacuated and it took 200 firemen all night to stop the blaze spreading.

They hosed down houses to keep them cool as 150,000 gallons of paint resin sent flames shooting 150 feet high. A fire brigade officer said: 'It was a hell of a situation. Drums were taking off like rockets.

'We had to work flat out to stop the flames spreading to other buildings. Luckily there was no wind or it could have been a lot worse.'

The dead driver, Mr Michael Grady, 40, of Bowness Road, Little Lever, Bolton, was found as firemen doused downed the red-hot metal drums.

The initial blast blew grandfather Norman Halsall through a window, his clothes ablaze.

Blistered

Chris Mather, 24, came to his aid. 'I managed to put the flames out with my hands,' he said. 'He was in a terrible state.'

Mr Halsall, 46, was said to be 'improving' at Tame-

DEATH BLAST

like rockets

side Hospital.

Two drums landed on the roof of conservationist Frank Swallow, who has campaigned for five years for the plant to be closed. The heat blew out windows and blistered paint-work on his house, just 20ft from the factory.

Mr Swallow, 61, said: 'The village will not allow the factory to open again. This is a conservation area and almost everyone in the village signed a petition in 1979 demanding it should be closed.

'We always knew this would happen. Next time, this village could be wiped out.'

Damage

Mr Swallow claimed that when he wrote to the factory inspectorate they replied that there were no grounds to shut the factory. Their letter said: 'In the event of fire, there should be no risk to adjacent property.'

Mr Ken Rae, chairman of Tameside council's environmental health committee, said: 'I want this factory and its owners out of the village.'

Factory boss George Molyneaux, 38, said: 'The cause of the fire is not known but I hope to be operating again in six months.' Damage was estimated at £500,000.

from *The Daily Mail*

Questions

1 Sum up the factual details of this incident.
2 What use has been made of headlines and subheadings in these two articles?
3 Look at the following carefully. Compare the words used in each article and explain the effects of the choices.

'the fire at the chemical factory' (*The Guardian*)
'the massive chemical plant explosion' (*Daily Mail*)

'Strange drums exploded' (*The Guardian*)
'drums were taking off like rockets' (*Daily Mail*)

'the injured man, a process worker Mr Norman Halsall, was said to be seriously ill in hospital' (*The Guardian*)
'the initial blast blew grandfather Norman Halsall through a window his clothes ablaze' and 'turned a process worker into a human fireball' (*Daily Mail*)

'local people have been concerned about the chemical drums' (*The Guardian*)
'they accused the Government officials of ignoring their warnings of a holocaust' (*Daily Mail*)

4 The headline of the *Daily Mail* article is
AFTERMATH OF DEATH BLAST
and *The Guardian*
CHEMICAL BLAZE PROMPTS INQUIRY INTO SAFETY.
How accurate and appropriate are these headlines in introducing the articles which accompany them? What is the effect achieved by the choice of words in each case?
5 Both writers report the actual words of people involved in the incident. By referring to specific speeches, explain what the effect of this is? Why, do you think, the *Daily Mail* writer does this more than *The Guardian* writer?
6 What do the stories of Mr Chris Mather and Mr Frank Swallow add to the *Daily Mail* article? Why has the writer included them?
7 What extra information does *The Guardian* writer add to the original story? What seems to concern him about the incident?
8 Write a paragraph summing up the presentation and style of each of these articles.

Practice work

Either

Write an article for a newspaper or magazine about the changing face of your environment.

Or

Write an article for a newspaper or magazine about the contribution young people in your area have made to the life of the community.

Before you begin writing, collect the necessary facts and choose the style for the article.

Choosing the tone

> The tone is the way in which you express yourself and the attitude you show. The tone you choose must be appropriate to your purpose.
> Read the following article carefully.

Yugoslavia – The Sunny Adriatic

The Yugoslav Adriatic Coast stretches from Ankaran on the Yugoslav-Italian frontier down to Ulcinj, close to the Albanian border. A region of exceptional scenic beauty enjoying a delightful sunny climate almost all year round, it offers the visitor wonderful bathing, abundant greenery, charming old towns and quiet villages, art treasures and historical monuments. As such, it ranks among the most attractive parts of the Mediterranean.

This is one of the most indented coasts in Europe: 628 kilometres in length as the crow flies, it has an actual shoreline of 2,092 km. The special attraction of the Yugoslav Adriatic is its proverbial thousand islands. Though many, of course, are very tiny and uninhabited, large ones with their picturesque towns are popular tourist centres with new hotels, lovely beaches and tranquil pine-fringed bays.

The lovely rugged coast of Istria in the north has countless small coves backed by pines, a mild climate, many picturesque coastal towns and a very attractive hinterland of rolling green hills. A string of pretty resorts edges the Kvarner Bay on the eastern coast of the Istrian peninsula. From here ferries ply to the islands of Cres, Krk, Rab and Losinj.

The southern Adriatic Coast, running from Neretva to Ulcinj, has very few islands but lovely sandy beaches, a crystal-clear sea and an exceptionally pleasant climate, making it possible to swim until late October. In this region lies Dubrovnik, sometimes called Yugoslavia's Ambassador to Tourism. This remarkable city alone would make a visit to the southern Adriatic worthwhile. But there is much else besides: the breathtaking Gulf of Boka Kotorska – the only real fjord in southern Europe, the quaint walled town of Budva, flower-filled Herceg-Novi the luxurious hotel-village of Sveti Stefan, pretty Petrovac, and the 12-kilometre-long sandy beaches of Ulcinj.

And don't forget that you will be welcomed on the Yugoslav Adriatic by a proud, warm and hospitable people who know how to receive guests, win your heart, and generously repay every kind word. Everyone will greet you sincerely with the words:

DOBRO DOSLI! WELCOME!

Questions

1 What is the writer's purpose in writing this article?
2 What is the tone of the article?
3 Explain how each of the following expressions adds to the tone.
'a region of exceptional scenic beauty'
'enjoying a delightful sunny climate almost all year round'
'wonderful bathing'
'abundant greenery'
'ranks among the most attractive parts of the Mediterranean'
'are very tiny and uninhabited, large ones with their picturesque towns'
'lovely beaches and tranquil pine-fringed bays'
'crystal-clear sea'
'a string of pretty resorts edges the Kvarner Bay'
'DOBRI DOSLI! WELCOME!'

Practice work

Write an article about your school buildings and grounds using the same style and tone as the article on Yugoslavia.

Practice work

Either

Rewrite each letter keeping the same information but using a more appropriate tone.

Or

Write either of the following letters setting it out properly, sticking to the point and using the correct tone.

You are not satisfied with your purchase. Write a letter making your complaint and asking for your money back.

The gas fire which you ordered does not suit your room. Write a letter explaining this and asking if it could be exchanged for another type.

Read the following letters, written in response to an article by Angela Rush about the nuclear threat.

Learning to Live at Peace in a Nuclear Age

1 I am listening to Angela Rush's impassioned plea about the nuclear threat (Open Space, 10 Sept) and I can do something – and so can she. When fear turns into anger (as it did in my case) it is amazing how much energy is released to spend on trying to ensure that our children have a future.

For a start, she can join with all those people who feel the way she does, on the CND march in London on 24 October. Then I suggest she buys a copy of E P Thompson's *Protest and Survive*, joins her local anti-missile group or starts one, writes to her MP informing him that she will not vote for him unless his policy is for getting rid of nuclear weapons on our soil and particularly for not allowing Cruise missiles to be sited here. She could get up a petition against Cruise, talk to her friends about it – in some way or another everyone can help in the campaign to stop Cruise missiles coming to Britain.

I'm terrified but at least I am using all that strong feeling in trying to do something about the situation.

2 In answer to Angela Rush who is constantly terrified of the bomb threat, 20 years ago I felt the same, and so did all the children I was teaching the day the Russians tested a bomb and they admitted themselves they did not know what the result would be. We all felt the world might end by lunchtime.

I have come to several conclusions which have helped me and may help Angela and others who feel as she does. First, we all know that we are going to die eventually, we imagine that for us it is going to be a long time ahead, and that it will be a peaceful end.

If we lived our whole lives in terror of this event, fear would prevent us from doing anything constructive at all. Suicide is no escape from death. Worry would drive millions insane, so we learn to live with it and accept it, or don't even think about it, and carry on leading our lives in the best way we can.

Second, Angela's child (or any other newborn baby) may be the very one to solve the problem of the bomb, or do a great deal towards solving it. By not bringing him/her into this 'world without hope' she may be withholding a solution that could save millions of lives.

Third, a friend pointed out to me that every child born today is born completely untaught in the ways of good or evil. Let us ignore the law of averages for a moment and suppose that everyone grows up to be good and peace loving, and brings up their children the same way. Two generations and the people who want evil and war would no longer exist. There would be no need to worry about the bombs, no one would want it. Unlikely, I know, but I like to think it is possible.

Fourth, Angela may not be in the least religious, but it helps me when I remember that God made all this beautiful world and everything in it.

I honestly believe that prayer is the strongest 'weapon' for peace in the world, and that through consistent, sincere prayer and listening quietly for answers, people will be led to take the practical measures necessary to ensure earthly peace and plenty.

3 Angela Rush and Molly Lisseter are certainly not alone in their feelings of terror and dismay over the threat of nuclear war. The Women's March for Life on Earth, a group of ordinary women from all over Britain (and some men and children too), have walked 110 miles from Cardiff to the RAF base at Greenham Common, Newbury, to protest against the base's proposal as a Cruise missile site. In desperation over the lack of media coverage and public response, four of these women chained themselves to the fence at the entrance gate when they arrived at the base on 5 September and announced their intention to stay there until there is a public television debate on the issue.

No one can afford to be complacent about nuclear war. We are all one people on one planet. We must all demand a stop to this insanity. Four women are still chained to the fence at Greenham Common. Come out and give them your support!

Questions

1   What do we learn from these letters about the content of Angela Rush's article?
2   How would you describe the tone and purpose of each letter?
3   Sum up the points being made in each letter. Which writer do you think expresses his/her case most effectively and why?

Practice work

Write a letter to a newspaper or magazine in response to an article which appeared on one of the following subjects. Choose an appropriate tone for your letter.

HOW SHOPS SUCK YOU INTO SPENDING

Shoppers beware! There's a scheming mind behind every tempting store display.

FOR PEACE SAKE, MARCH!

"Why not join the march for a nuclear-free Europe?"

NEW STYLE FAMILIES

Family life is going through a period of change, says Tom Crabtree, but with hard work, good will and imagination we can make sure it survives · · · · and improves

HOMEWORK –
IS IT A GOOD IDEA?

Why clever children fail in school

It's quite common to find a gifted child doing badly at school, but why does this happen? Dr A Joseph Burstein suggests possible reasons

Practice work In order to write about one of the following you need **to use the skills** you have practised in this section. You need to collect the necessary facts and express them clearly. The ideas must be developed and organised in the most appropriate way. You will also need to think about the tone you wish to use.

Do-it-yourself
Independent Television Networks
Video recorders
Litter
Public transport
Health and beauty
Examinations
Fashion
Local social and leisure facilities
How to succeed at . . . . . .

Extracts used

Index